THE LIFE
AND SPIRIT OF
THOMAS AQUINAS

L. H. PETITOT, O.P.

THE LIFE
AND SPIRIT OF
THOMAS AQUINAS

Translated by
Cyprian Burke, O.P.

THE PRIORY PRESS, CHICAGO, ILL.

This book is a translation of *La Vie Integrale de St. Thomas d'Aquin* and of "La Mort de St. Thomas d'Aquin," an article which appeared in *La Vie Spirituelle*. Both the book and the article were published by Les Éditions du Cerf, Paris.

Revisores Ordinis: Augustine Rock, O.P., S.T.D.; Bernard O'Riley, O.P. *Imprimi potest*: Gilbert J. Graham, O.P., Provincial. *Nihil obstat*: Augustine Rock, O.P., S.T.D.; Bernard O'Riley, O.P., Censores Deputati. *Imprimatur*: ✠ John P. Cody, Archbishop of Chicago, August 23, 1966.

PREFACE

This biography of St. Thomas Aquinas was published forty years ago. The works written since that time on the life and teaching of the great Doctor have certainly deepened our knowledge of his personality and his work; far from diminishing, they have confirmed the fundamental intuition of Père Petitot's work, which was already indicated by the book's success (eleven editions in fifteen years).

Père Petitot reacted strongly against the way in which the lives of famous men, thinkers, and rulers were written in his day. This was probably especially true of the lives of Christian saints. On the one hand, scholars scrutinized the events and circumstances of a man's life, recorded in the documents of the time, with a purely objective precision. On the other hand, pious authors developed long praises of the virtues and edifying miracles of a saint's life. And if he happened to be a Master or Doctor of the faith, they analyzed the unchanging and abstract truth of his philosophical and theological teachings, as if the biographers were interested only in past polemics without pointing out their value. Finally, they separated Christian life into two distinct domains: the ascetic, as a model for all, and the mystical, more or less reserved for the initiated.

Historians, psychologists, sociologists, theologians, and preachers have reacted against this piecemeal method, which would defeat the reality of life and thought. They not only desired to reintroduce into the study of men of the past the external context, but also the profound unity they found there. Certainly the normal distinction of epistemological levels and formal objects must be observed, so that the work will be well ordered. But the permanence of truth and spiritual values is in no way threatened by an analysis of the current trends, the influence of the times, and the evolution of cultures.

The case of St. Thomas is particularly significant. To analyze the historical and sociological conditions of his work is the best way of measuring the truth of his teaching in relationship to its place in civilization and in the course of theological development. We find this realism again today, and understand better how the Word of God is incarnate in the history of humanity, in the world of space and time. Theology should not be a closed chapel in the midst of men, but a faithful expression and elaboration of the Word of God in a mature faith.

Such was the genius of the work of St. Thomas Aquinas.

M. D. Chenu, O.P.
Paris, April 25, 1966

INTRODUCTION

The title of this little work: *The Life and Spirit of Thomas Aquinas,* may at first appear to the reader as rather pretentious or at least puzzling. Although it is obvious that I cannot say everything about St. Thomas in such a small work, we can still call it an *integral* life of the Angelic Doctor, but in a restricted and consequently more precise sense.

By integral I do not mean one part contributing to the whole, but only that which is indispensable for normal activity. In this sense arms and hands can be considered integral parts of the human body. Lesser parts contribute to its perfection, but they are not integral in our use of the word.

Likewise in the moral order, the heart, feelings, and emotions are obviously integral parts of the human personality. When a person decides to study the lives of certain philosophers, like Aristotle, Plato, Pascal, or St. Thomas, he is sometimes led to consider them from an exclusively human point of view, without giving the rightful place to their spiritual and mystical life. On the other hand, when other biographers study the lives of saints, apostles, or mystics, like Dominic, Theresa of Avila, Francis de Sales, or Theresa of Lisieux, they do not place intellectual activity in its proper perspective. As a consequence, many biographies reflect the prejudices of their authors, and therefore do not present an integral view of the personality.

Life is complex; it is essentially synthetic. Besides his intelligence, man is endowed with a will, a faculty of acting, of feeling. An integral view of man must emphasize the proportional and reciprocal influence of the intellect, will, and religious feeling. This is the task I have set in this biography of St. Thomas. I do not mean to say that our principal faculties are not relatively independent and autonomous. This is a fact of experience that is easy to establish. As St. John of the Cross says: "It is possible to know little and love much, just as it is possible to have vast knowledge and love little." We must guard against establishing too strict a mutual dependence between the faculties. This independence of our faculties or powers is sometimes so great that it seems that they are fundamentally opposed, whereas they really condition one another. It is possible that an outstanding speculative theologian may not be as zealous an apostle or tender a mystic, so that his integral growth would consist precisely in the synthesis of contrary or complementary qualities. This is what Pascal meant when he said: "An adequate evaluation of personality must include all contrarieties, for it is not sufficient to make a list of compatible qualities without adding the contrary ones."

For twenty years, I have endeavored to apply this first principle of integralism, that is, synthesizing all truths, faculties, virtues, and contrary, contradictory, or complementary gifts, while maintaining their relative autonomy. These twenty years were an era of lively discussions about the relative role played by the intelligence, will, action, and emotion in finding the true religion. At the same time my confrere, Père de Poulpiquet, was writing about his work on the integral object of apologetics. Most of us had read and studied closely the important work of Maurice Blondel, *L'Action*. There was a great deal of discussion at that time about immanence and integral teaching. It was then that I began the study of integralism in Pascal. I have also attempted to show that certain contemporary authors, while maintaining correctly the mutual dependence of our faculties, do not respect their relative autonomy. Since then, I have adopted this theory of integralism even into our purely historical studies. But I have sometimes been misunderstood.

The first time that I spoke of the relative independence of the parts of a vital synthesis (in a work on integral apologetics), I received a rather admirably frank response: "They do not give an account of the relative independence of arguments which must form a vital synthesis." Later, when I had the boldness to speak of positive contradictions in the life of St. Theresa of Lisieux, certain persons thought that these expressions were strange and out of place. There were others who understood; and one such person, a professor at Louvain, noted correctly that the study, *Saint Theresa of Lisieux*, was only a particular application of the thesis on the method of integralism presented in my *Introduction à la philosophie classique.*

The use of this method in the life of St. Thomas Aquinas accounts for the success of the book. Despite its omissions and imperfections, it sold out rapidly. What I have tried to do is to show in a living synthesis the harmonious union of the intellectual, mystical, ascetic, and apostolic life in the personality who might well be called the greatest Doctor of the Church.

No informed person could doubt that Thomas was above all an incredible genius. In his apostolate and mystical life, he was always what would today be called intellectual. His preaching ordinarily reproduced or prolonged his doctrinal teaching in more accessible and edifying forms. His prayers, his ecstasies were more often an intellectual than affective contemplation. In the composition of tracts, and particularly of the *Summa Theologiae*, his method of investigation and exposition is rigorously rational. The Augustinians, both ancient and modern, have rather wrongly reproached him for this. The Jansenists have unjustly accused him of rationalism.

It is true that Thomas said that the intellect is autonomous in its domain, that it must follow its own proper laws, proceed logically by principles and conclusions without being detoured by considerations of expediency, edification, or emotion. In this sense, he adopted a precise and scientific method in his theological works. But Thomas knew, wrote in his *Summa,* and preached in the pulpit that the human intellect, left to itself, is very weak and at the mercy of the senses.* He was fully aware that reason must be kept on the right path by a respect for tradition and docility to the direction of the Church. Finally, he stated that to be understood integrally, divine truths must not be merely learned or apprehended by the intellect but they must be felt by the heart, lived, or in his own words, "suffered."

It would be inaccurate to picture St. Thomas as a logician or theologian, who proceeds from principles given once and for all by revelation, applying himself to strict reasoning, without considering anything other than the correctness of his argumentation. So as not to wander at random, Thomas most prudently verified his conclusions by comparing them with the teaching of the Fathers and the Church. To produce a way of life, of Christian and supernatural life, he prayed much; he prayed without ceasing.

*See below, Chapter II, on the sermon of the *Vetula,* and also P. Kuhn, *Saint Thomas d'Aquin, prédicateur.*

His extreme prudence, docility, and profound piety did not prevent him from realizing the urgent need for doctrinal reform if souls were to be saved. He ventured to begin, to pursue, and to finish this doctrinal revival despite the attacks and fainthearted fears of certain traditionalists, some of whom were his own fellow Dominicans.

Thomistic teaching is not only the work of reason reasoning, but of docility, humility, patience, strength, magnanimity, and sanctity. We should not let ourselves be deceived by the dialectic in which it was conceived or by the framework in which it is expressed. This logical form is less essential to the substance of Thomistic teaching than is usually thought. Outstanding Thomistic theologians have presented theses in a coherent literary or even oratorical discourse without resorting to syllogistic, logical, or dialectical expressions. We cannot say the same of geometry which is essentially and exclusively a reasoning process.

Siger of Brabant, Boethius of Dacia, and the Averroists did not err because they lacked a sufficient knowledge of the laws of logic and dialectic. On the contrary, they were concise and excellent logicians. They were literally past masters of dialectic. And although they had been more familiar with this kind of intellectual fencing, and although they had made a close grammatical exegesis of the Greek text of Aristotle (which they had memorized in its entirety), with all this erudition, they were foiled by a specious verisimilitude and logic.

What they especially lacked was not the discursive intelligence, the mathematical spirit, documentation, or learning, but a respect for tradition and a submission to the spirit and the rule of faith, to the *magisterium* of the Church. What they lacked was commonsense, judgment, and the ability to distinguish the false from the true.

This feeling, this judgment, this intuition into truth which detects error in moral, philosophical, theological, and doctrinal questions, and then exposes it, was possessed in an outstanding degree by St. Thomas. His was an entirely different frame of mind from the geometrical or dialectical. It is not by racking our brains with dialectical exercises, but rather by striving to justify ourselves each day, by practicing justice in the spiritual sense spoken of in the Bible, that we can acquire this justice of soul, particularly in the complex questions of theodicy, morals, and revealed theology. For this reason, I have tried to show how the work of justification or salvation held the most prominent place in the life of St. Thomas, and that it contributed more to the writing of the *Summa* than is usually thought.

After considering how this sanctification of the Angelic Doctor is distinct but inseparable from his work, and how it is reintegrated, we must show how the ascetic and mystical life of our Saint contributed to the elaboration of his theology. I have tried to indicate how his asceticism was very much like that of the Desert Fathers, while being at the same time distinctly intellectual. As St. John of the Cross, Tauler, and others put it when commenting on the Gospel text: *Nemo potest duobus dominis servire.* Christian asceticism is based on the principle that two incompatible activities cannot survive at the same time in the same person. The more our work is generous and elevated and the more we are entirely absorbed in it, the more it will begin to exclude inferior and secondary preoccupations. First, I have noted that St. Thomas was vigilant in restraining his senses and emotions, mortifying his conversations, visits, and superfluous relationships. Aware of his special vocation, which was to become an outstanding theologian, he mortified all his literary, artistic, and administrative aptitudes. He was not preoccupied with politics or the administration of his Order. He would not agree to being made a cardinal. He was not a man of half-measures, nor was he implicated in intrigues.

St. Thomas specialized in his work as a theologian, returning again and again to the same questions. His outstanding example is a sign and worthy lesson for us, who, contaminated by the contagion of our century, are so often disquieted and unable to devote ourselves to the study of a single subject. It may be that the difficult circumstances in which we struggle have led us to disperse our efforts. We apply ourselves successively to very different tasks. We have been what might be called dilettantes. Whether this diffusion is our own fault or not, it has been very detrimental to us. We hope that the young learn from our unfortunate experiences. I am not saying that they should specialize too early. This is a situation where we must reconcile contraries. Much varied and diverse experience is useful and even indispensable to the creation of a philosophy of life. But it is necessary that all this knowledge and experience be unified by one idea, be oriented in a single direction.

The unavoidable law which is useless to argue against, which will judge us if we do not submit to it, was promulgated for centuries in the form of the well-known saying: *Timeo hominem unius libri.* In order to emerge from honorable mediocrity, to excel, it is necessary to apply oneself to a single discipline, to a single study. Those who are not courageous enough to limit themselves, to die to many things, who spread their activity in divergent directions, will be only second-rate. No doubt they will have accomplished a great deal, but it is not sufficient for those who can do more. An outstanding scholar who concentrates his efforts in a long career in one field of study and attains the top place, makes us realize that certain brilliant intellects only dissipate their potentialities by thinking that they lack courage and depth, and are incapable of defending themselves against the enticements of many requests coming from without. This weakness of mind and will cannot but result in a certain anxiety.

However, it seems to me that, if these gifted minds were put on their guard against the ever-growing dangers of unrest and dissipation, significant works of great scope and of the first order would be produced by Catholic writers in ever-increasing numbers. It is necessary to repeat that this great Saint, this distinguished Doctor was detached from all that glittered, from all that was ephemeral, from all which did not concern him, in order that he might devote himself to his theological and apologetical work.

In the early editions, I spoke of all I owe to the revealing work of Père Mandonnet on St. Thomas Aquinas, Siger of Brabant, and Averroism. I want to thank the critics whose observations were so benevolent. Some of them have asked me to add a summary of the teaching of St. Thomas to this little book, with notes or appendices on the many questions of the plurality of forms and creation *ab aeterno*. Such studies would encumber this volume. Moreover they have already been discussed in the works of P. Sertillanges, M. Maritain, and M. Gilson. I have limited myself to correcting those errors and mistakes which the critics have indicated. My purpose has been, and remains, to present the public with an unimposing popularization of the integral life of St. Thomas.

CONTENTS

THE LIFE
AND SPIRIT OF
THOMAS AQUINAS

One: YOUTH AND VOCATION

Ordinarily, medieval chronicles and biographies relate an edifying incident from the infancy and early childhood of a saint. These accounts, which usually have some foundation in fact, are intended to symbolize an outstanding characteristic the Saint would develop later in life. Theresa of Avila and her brother Rodriguez, for example, left their home to be martyrs in the land of the Moors. We read of two such incidents in the early years of the life of St. Thomas.

William of Tocco, the Saint's principal biographer, relates the first event.

Once his mother and some other women went to the baths at Naples. They went off leaving the infant with his nurse. When the nurse put the child down in the room where she usually sat, he grabbed hold of a piece of parchment that was lying in the room. The nurse tried to open the hand which held the paper, to make him drop it. The child cried so loudly however, that she let him keep it, washing him with his hand closed. When his mother came back to the child, she forced him to open his hand, and found the *Ave Maria* written on the piece of parchment.

Contrary to a common accusation, the author did not say that Thomas chewed and swallowed the paper. He merely adds: "When the child began to cry again for one reason or another, he could be quieted only by giving him the piece of parchment, which he put into his mouth." The account is intended to symbolize Thomas' devotion to the Mother of God, a devotion which would later lead him to write a commentary on the *Ave Maria*. We shall find more convincing examples of his tenacity later on.

The second incident occurred when Thomas was little more than five years old. While he was at the Benedictine school of Monte Cassino, Thomas is said to have frequently repeated the primordial question, "Who is God?" In the words of William of Tocco, this was truly an omen of the whole life and theological career of a man who would be called the greatest of Christian doctors. One day, shortly before his death, the Saint received the final answer to this childhood question. After that day, the pen fell from his hand, never to be taken up again.

In this first chapter, we will examine the Saint's vocation in the widest sense of that term. Rarely does a person set aside by Divine Providence attain, before the age of twenty-five, complete awareness of the mission given him. Such was probably the case with regard to St. Thomas; hence these first twenty-five years must be investigated.

We have mentioned that Thomas lived in the Benedictine monastery of Monte Cassino as a young boy. Historians have passionately debated his status during these years. Was Thomas "vowed" to the Order of St. Benedict by his parents? Was he vested in the Benedictine habit or was he merely a boarding student?

In the past, Dominican historians have been violently opposed to the hypothesis of Thomas' oblature and vestition. They established their arguments on three principal facts. First, the custom of consecrating small children to a Religious Order had been abolished, especially in the Abbey of Monte Cassino, before the end of the twelfth century. Mabillon points this out, and the fact is certain. It would be necessary, therefore, to admit an exception in the case of St. Thomas.

Moreover, a child consecrated to a Religious Order belonged to the monastery. We know that St. Thomas continued to recognize parental authority, and when he took the Dominican habit, the Abbot of Monte Cassino did not seem to raise the least protest or complaint.

Finally, the Saint's first biographers, Tolomeo of Lucca and William of Tocco, state clearly that the child had been a boarder at Monte Cassino under the care of a special tutor. This was the general practice with the children of nobles educated at the abbey. For this reason, Echard, Touron, and others, while recognizing that the family intended

to make Thomas the Abbot of Monte Cassino, have
rejected the idea of an oblature and vestition. Their
thesis still appears to us to be tenable today.[1]

Dominican scholars, perhaps because of an excessive family spirit, have opposed the idea of St.
Thomas dressed in the Benedictine habit. Yet, if
we get some idea of the monastic history of the
Middle Ages, and read the testimony of the witnesses without prejudice, we are inclined to believe
that the child was an oblate and received the "black
habit" and tonsure. The evidence of Bartholomew
of Capua, a lawyer and secretary of the King of
Sicily, is rather convincing in this matter: "Pater

[1]Tolomeo of Lucca wrote: "Hic nutritus in sua pueritia
in abbatia Montis Cassini, qui sunt monachi et secundum
morem nobilium illius patria . . . habens semper secum spe-
cialem magistrum more nobilium regionis . . ." (*Hist. Eccl.*,
XXII, cap. XX). William of Tocco says almost the same
thing, but with less precision: "Cum autem praedictus puer-
lus coepisset in dicto monasterio sub disciplina Magistri
diligentius educare . . ." (cf. Bollandists, *Acta Sanctorum*
[VII Mars], I, p. 658). For information concerning documentation in St. Thomas, the *Bibliographie Thomiste* is both
accessible and indispensable. It contains complete information on the Saint, including articles, sources, studies, pane-
gyrics, etc. This valuable work ought to be made available
in all libraries. In this present study we will cite most often
Tolomeo of Lucca, William of Tocco, and the witnesses at
the process of canonization. Tolomeo of Lucca and William
of Tocco were disciples of the Saint. William of Tocco was
one of the inquisitors assigned to receive the testimonies of
the witnesses, and served as the principal promotor for the
canonization of the Saint. His authority is greatest when
he relates particular traits and events in the Saint's life. Since
there was little interest in dates among medieval biographers,
we must always relate their chronology to the more certain
events in the history of popes, emperors, and Religious Orders.

dicti fr. Thomae monachavit eum puerum." The expression *monachavit* is as significant as it is ungrammatical, for the English translation of the statement reads: "The father of the said brother Thomas 'monked' him [i.e., made him a monk], when he was just a child." This term alone is enough for us to get some notion of the whole train of ceremonies, rites, and obligations which the oblature carries with it.[2]

There is a legend which substantiates the lawyer's evidence. In medieval lives of saints, it is quite common to read of an old white-bearded hermit playing the role of Simeon at the birth of a saint and predicting the child's future. He is a necessary character, part of the scenery. In our story, the good hermit is called Fra Bonus. He came to the mother and said:

Rejoice, noble lady, for you have conceived and you will bear a son, and you will call him Thomas. You and your husband will decide to make him a monk in the monastery of Monte Cassino in order to profit from the rich revenues of the abbey and the supreme authority of your son's office. But God has ordained otherwise, for he will be a Brother of the Order of Preachers. And he will excel so much in learning and holiness that no one will equal him.[3]

[2]Consult the articles by Père Mandonnet in the *Revue des Jeunes*, May and June 1919, and January 25 and March 10, 1920. These studies are very important. They bring many points up to date. We especially recommend them to the reader who is interested in the childhood and youth of St. Thomas.

[3]Bollandists, *Acta Sanctorum* (VII Mars), I, p. 657.

The hermit certainly saw far into the future, but he was familiar with the customs of his own time, and knew very well that the Lords of Aquino would not hesitate to "monk" their own son even before he had reached the age of reason, in order to appropriate the rich revenues of the immense neighboring abbey.

Hence, at the age of five, as soon as the child had passed from the care of his nurse and mother, the family brought him to the abbey in great pomp, where his parents offered him graciously to God: "Libenter Deo offerunt." We can picture Thomas as a little Benedictine monk, dressed with the black robe and scapular, pulling the pointed hood of the habit over his head like a candle extinguisher when he passed through the cloisters. He served Mass in the church, filled various functions in the processions and ceremonies, learned to read Latin, to chant the Psalms, and to sing from the enormous antiphonary placed in the middle of the choir where he was assigned to turn pages. The life of this little Eliah was very happy. Thomas was doted on by the monks and was the joy and hope of the abbey.

The chronicler tells us that Thomas' parents offered their child "*libenter*," that is, in a disinterested manner. Without questioning the religious motives of the donors, we need only recall the strong and forthright frankness of Fra Bonus: "You hope that, by making your son Abbot of Monte Cassino, you will participate in the rich revenues of the monastery (*ad magnos ipsius monasterii reditus pervenire . . .*)." Certainly family interest, ambition, passion for grandeur, and even diplomacy played an important part in the offering of Thomas to God.

Being Abbot of Monte Cassino was no small honor. Thomas of Cantimpré assures us that the abbey was the most important in Abulia and Compania. It included seven dioceses, and the abbot exercised episcopal rank. The monastery, a center of vast territorial power, had been transformed into a fortress by necessity. The previous year, 1229, the monks withstood a strong siege against Emperor Frederick II, who was aided very effectively by the Count of Aquino. The abbey was finally captured and sacked.

The family of Aquino lived in a nearby fortress lodged at the peak of a high hill among the arid slopes (which gave it the name "Roccasecca"). The Counts of Aquino were important nobles. Thomas' grandfather served as the lieutenant general of Frederick Barbarossa, who rewarded him with the hand of his sister, Frances of Souabia. St. Thomas, then, was the grandson of Frederick Barbarossa's sister. His two brothers, Reginald and Landulf, lieutenants in the army of Frederick II, worthily continued the military traditions of a family which had been warriors from time immemorial. The monks of Monte Cassino knew this tradition well, for only too often the Counts of Aquino had ransomed their monastery. As we have just seen, the Saint's father, Landulf, had prepared the siege, and openly cooperated in the capture of the monastery in 1229.

In 1230, however, peace was concluded between Pope Gregory IX and Emperor Frederick II, in the nearby city of San Germano. One of the results of the treaty was the oblature of young Thomas, who had just reached the age of five years. Since a noble family would not present its son without offering a princely gift in the form of a dowry, Count Landulf bestowed upon the abbey twenty ounces of gold, a considerable sum for the time. It is evident that the oblature of little Thomas and the offering destined to reconstruct the abbot's lodgings were a pledge of peace. While the monks would be safe under the protection of the House of Aquino, the family would be helped in the cultivation of its lands by the aid of the religious and the revenues of their future abbot, Thomas Aquinas. Thomas, the youthful Benedictine monk, was a pledge of peace for all—the religious, his family, and the entire region.

By the age of ten he could read and write; he studied the first elements of the Latin language, arithmetic, and grammar. At thirteen he had memorized a great part of the Psalter, the Gospels, and the Epistles of St. Paul. His tutor made him translate the writings of the Fathers, the sermons of St. Gregory, the letters of St. Jerome, and excerpts from the writings of St. Augustine. In the library of the abbey, he learned to know and to love books and manuscripts.

The length of his schooling in the monastery is uncertain. Generally, the Dominican historians who dispute the Benedictine oblature are eager to get him out of the abbey. They claim that he was removed from the monastery when he was eleven in order to be sent to the University of Naples. Yet it is more probable that he remained in the abbey until his fourteenth year. It is obvious that Thomas' Benedictine education would have left a deeper indelible mark on his mind and heart if he had been an oblate until his fourteenth year, and not just a boarder until his eleventh year. During the whole of his childhood and the beginnings of his adolescence, St. Thomas breathed the profoundly spiritual and mystical atmosphere which pervaded the Benedictine abbey and its life: the cloister arches, the nave of the church, the dark and beautiful stained glass windows, the Gregorian melodies, and the magnificent and stately ceremonies. Already he must have been deeply impressed by sacred music. He would always keep his taste and feeling for the liturgy, and in his teaching he carefully safeguarded the rights of art and humanism. Certainly the early and lengthy Benedictine education inculcated in the Angelic Doctor a respect for ideal and pure beauty, poetry and religious art.

It might seem surprising that a young man destined to be made Abbot of Monte Cassino should be sent to study at the University of Naples. Such a decision was contrary to the most hallowed of ancient monastic customs. William of Tocco writes that the abbot counseled this change. Only a century earlier, the great reformer, Bernard of Clairvaux, would never have tolerated such a decision. A man likely to be appointed abbot should have remained in his monastery under the care of the pious and learned monks entrusted with his formation. Sending such a young person to the city of Naples could only lead to his perdition. It is likely that Thomas would have remained at Monte Cassino had there not been several external developments necessitating his departure.

The most pressing was the renewed hostilities between Frederick II and the Pope. The Emperor considered the Abbey of Monte Cassino as a primary means of papal influence, and demanded that the monks be evicted. These events followed shortly after the excommunication of Frederick by Gregory IX on March 20, 1239. At this time, Thomas returned to his family, leaving his Benedictine habit behind. He had passed his fourteenth year.

Nevertheless these events which forced Thomas to return to his father's home would not necessarily explain why he was sent to study at the University of Naples. Thomas' parents had by no means given up their ambition to see Thomas as Abbot of Monte

Cassino. The reasons for this decision must be sought elsewhere.

At this time, a powerful scientific, philosophical, and theological movement was being propagated in Christianity. Two Lateran Councils, as well as Popes Innocent III, Honorius III, and Gregory IX, ordered the clergy to take up higher studies. Schools and universities were founded in almost every large city. Religious Orders, even the contemplative Cistercians and Benedictines, felt themselves carried forward by the very force of this current. There would come a day when a monk would rarely become an abbot unless he were a doctor of theology; hence Thomas' family felt the urgency of sending him to the University of Naples.

The final reason is subjective and decisive. This young man was exceptionally, even extraordinarily, inclined to study. As is frequently the case with students who are more intelligent than skillful, he was only a mediocre penman. It seems that he possessed hardly any aptitudes for physical and military exercises, and he did not like violent and noisy games. He was endowed with an incomparably acute intelligence and memory, and would retire willingly to read and reflect, beginning already, according to the chroniclers, to be a man of silence: "Jam incipiens taciturnus." He was obviously called to the ecclesiastical state, and since the abbey school was closed, there was no alternative but to send him to the University of Naples.

We know little about the life Thomas led as a student at Naples. William of Tocco tells us that a professor named Martin taught him logic and grammar, and Peter of Ireland taught him natural sciences. From the very beginning of his studies, the young man progressed with such exceptional speed that he astonished the masters and his fellow students. His fame, the biographer adds, spread throughout Naples.[4]

He was "gifted with such genius and such perception that he repeated his lessons with more insight and depth than that with which the masters first taught them." Undoubtedly he became a tutor, entrusted to explain the professors' theses to the younger students.

It was during his years at Naples that Thomas first encountered the Dominicans. It could hardly have been otherwise. The entire orientation of the life of these Friars Preachers was centered in study and doctrinal preaching. Soon after their establishment twenty years earlier, they entered the university cities of Europe and won immediate success as teachers and preachers. This thoroughly modern order met the needs of its time, and because of this, developed rapidly. Its growth in Christian Europe has been compared to an invasion. Five

[4]"Magistros et alios in admirationem adducebat, et per scholas celebris ejus fama volabat" ("He evoked the admiration of the masters and students, and his renown spread among the schools of Naples").

years earlier in Paris, during the winter trimester alone, seventy-two masters and students took the habit. St. Thomas, too, was exposed to the influence.

As was their custom, the Preachers established their convent and chapel at the center of the city, in the midst of the universities. In one of their halls, the Friars taught courses in theology. Each convent was obliged to be a school. The Dominicans lived among the students, doctors, preachers, and mendicants at the same time. They were monks in every sense of the word, with choral office, monastic observances, fast, abstinence, and a vow of poverty stricter than that practiced by the ancient orders. Thomas Aquinas found in the convent of the Preachers all that he had grown to love in the monastery of Monte Cassino. He was especially attracted by the new elements of preaching and teaching. To be a monk while preaching doctrine in church and teaching theology in a university was a life which combined all his desires, aspirations, and talents. Was it possible for him to join these Friars? Was he not committed to the Benedictines of Monte Cassino?

Thomas Aquinas contacted a Dominican, John of San Guiliano. There was no legal problem about his obligation to the Abbey of Monte Cassino. Thomas had not taken personal vows. According to the ordinances of recent popes, the oblature obliged to nothing. With regard to the ambitious plan of his family to make him Abbot of Monte

Cassino, his vocation, being a sacred thing, pertained to God and not to his parents. It was evident, however, that he would encounter violent opposition. Several years earlier, when the son of a noble family was received into the Order, the convent was nearly stormed by his father's armed servants. The Count of Aquino and Thomas' brothers were more formidable still. The Dominicans decided to wait until Thomas reached the canonical age of eighteen, and even then they would act only when an opportune occasion presented itself.[5]

On December 24, 1243, Count Landulf, Thomas' father, died. After the funeral, his brothers returned to the army of Frederick II. The Dominicans waited no longer to give their habit to the young man they would call Brother Thomas. The vestition ceremony took place in the first months of 1244, when the novice was nineteen years old. Clever means were taken to remove him from the effective authority of his family. The Master General of the Order of Preachers, John the Teuton, had to return to the General Chapter meeting in Bologna. He decided to take Brother Thomas to Bologna, where he would accompany the students of the Order leaving to study at the University of Paris. In this way,

[5]In 1237, Pope Gregory IX set eighteen as the valid age for profession. Certainly one could have taken the habit earlier, but this would have been useless and dangerous for Thomas Aquinas.

he would be saved from the vengeance of his family.[6]

No one has recorded the circumstances that upset these plans. The Dominicans of the convent at Naples had not reckoned on dealing with Thomas Aquinas' mother. Theodora of Naples, of the Caraccioli family, belonged to the fearsome race of Norman chiefs descended from Guiscard, Bohemond, and Tancred. A typical medieval countess, she was authoritative and haughty. There was no question in her mind that she must vindicate the supposed rights of her family as imperiously as would her husband, had he still been alive. When she learned of Thomas' departure from the convent of the Preachers, the Countess led a large party to reclaim him. The Dominicans told her truthfully that Thomas had left for Rome. More than any class, medieval nobility could not allow nor even conceive of a son or daughter marrying or entering religious life without the consent of the family. When Theodora arrived at Rome and knocked on the door of the convent of Santa Sabina, disappointment awaited her. The Master General, John the Teuton, had already set out for Bologna, taking Thomas in his custody. It is difficult to imagine the feelings of Theodora. Frustrated in her hope, outraged in her maternal authority, passionately

[6]Tolomeo of Lucca writes that the Master General of the Dominicans accompanied Brother Thomas from Naples: "Cum enim frater Johannes Teutonicus . . . de Neapoli fratrem Thomam educeret" (*Hist. Eccl.*, XXII, cap. XX).

irritated by the Dominicans and her son, she recoiled before any attempt at coercion. She dispatched a courier to her sons Reginald and Landulf, who were serving in the army of Frederick II, and told them to be on the lookout. If they found Thomas, they were to arrest him and return him to Roccasecca. These events took place in the spring, probably in May of 1244.[7]

[7]The chronology of the life of St. Thomas, like that of other personalities of the thirteenth century, is difficult to establish in even an approximate manner. The most certain date is that of his death, March 7, 1274. Some witnesses have stated that he was about forty-eight years old at the time. But William of Tocco, whose information is the most precise and trustworthy, writes that Thomas had completed his forty-ninth and had begun his fiftieth year. We would conclude from this that the Saint was born about March 7, 1225. A coincidence is pointed out by Père Mandonnet which might confirm this date. The gift of the twenty ounces of gold probably offered for Thomas' oblature was made in the year 1230. We know that the child had passed his fifth year, which would support 1225 as the year of his birth. As we have seen, the monks of Monte Cassino were evicted by Frederick II in 1239. Thomas was fourteen years old when he returned to the home of his father, shortly before he left for the University of Naples. According to the preceding account, it seems certain that, with Thomas' father dead, his mother Theodora acted on her authority as a widow. It would seem the vestition took place at the beginning of 1244. Shortly after receiving the habit, Brother Thomas was carried off to Acquapendente. The troops of Frederick II occupied this region only in 1243 and 1244. We also know that the Master General of the Order took Thomas in his company when he was returning to the General Chapter. The capture of the young Dominican must be placed, then, somewhere in May of 1244. These are the important dates of his youth. See Mandonnet, *Revue Thomiste* (1914), p. 625; and *Revue des Sciences philosophiques et theologiques* (1920), p. 142.

The Master General, with a little group of Religious including Brother Thomas, traveled toward Bologna along the road which passes through Viterbo, winding along Lake Bolsena. Frederick II's troups were positioned in this area, to the north at Acquapendente. Toward the middle of the day, since the sun was already hot, the pilgrims stopped near a spring. It felt good to rest on the grass and eat their frugal lunch in the shade of the trees. Swiftly moving horsemen appeared at the bend in the road leading toward Acquapendente. When they drew near the spring, Thomas recognized his brother Reginald. Suddenly he was surrounded. Despite the indignant appeals of the Master General and the other Religious, Brother Thomas was carried off by the soldiers. He was not hurt, but they tried to remove his monastic habit. Thomas, however, who was in his nineteenth year, was big and strong, and he kept his habit with the same stubbornness with which he grasped the piece of parchment as an infant. He wrapped his black cape around his body, gritting his teeth in silence. Neither his brother Reginald nor the soldiers could make him open his arms and give up his habit. For the time this was all he wanted. He docilely allowed himself to be placed on a horse and returned to his home.

William of Tocco assures us that Countess Theodora welcomed her returning son with great happiness. Even if he had not mentioned it, we would suspect her of experiencing the pleasure of success

and revenge. It is difficult to imagine the temperament of these great Italian families of the Middle
Ages. No chronicler or witness ever tells us that
Theodora pardoned her son. We hear nothing of
the mother trying to bend her child's will by tenderness. She used much cruder methods. Theodora
began by locking her son up in a fortress some
distance from the family castle. From time to time
she allowed her daughters, Marotta and Theodora,
to go and see the rebel. By affectionate arguments,
they strove to make him discard his Dominican
habit for that of the Benedictines, which he had
worn all his life and which his father had vowed
him to wear.[8]

The chroniclers like to picture Thomas as being
treated cruelly in the tower. Thomas of Cantimpré
writes of Thomas' torturers (*tortores*), who subject-
ed him to hunger and cold. William of Tocco says
that he was kept in the hold of the dungeon without
any light. These pious exaggerations are an attempt
to turn his captivity into a martyrdom. It is most
probable that Thomas was not treated inhumanly,
but only severely. Such a detention would have
been unbearable to a young cavalier, but it was
accepted very easily by a silent and holy novice.
Thomas Aquinas was perfectly suited for the er-

[8]"Ubi longo tempore vexatus est a habitum ordinis reli-
quendum, nec a sancto proposito averti potuit, sive minis,
sive blanditiis, seu quibuscumque modis, prohibentes ac-
cessum cujuscumque fratris" (Tolomeo of Lucca, *op. cit.*,
cap. XXI).

emitic and ascetic life. He began immediately on his own to live the regular life of a novice. The Dominicans of Naples, who were soon informed of his capture and imprisonment, tried to correspond with him. John of San Guiliano, his devoted director, came with two lay brothers to prowl about the fortress. They succeeded in getting messages and books to him. Seldom has there been a more stubborn battle between the natural and religious family to gain a son and brother.

His sisters, Theodora and Marotta, came often to talk with him. As docile and submissive daughters, they were their mother's representatives. They presented the arguments for the entire family. Why did Thomas insist on keeping the Dominican habit? They were not asking him to give up the religious state, but only to remain faithful to the Order of his childhood. This was only a question of color, a black robe in place of an entirely white one. The tradition and prosperity of the family depended on his making this sacrifice. We cannot imagine Thomas as being inhibited in his reply to these objections.

With the books that the Dominicans of Naples secured for him, Thomas studied Aristotle's *Sophisms* and the *Sentences* of Peter Lombard. He began a very profound study of the Bible. This is where he acquired that penetrating insight into the Scriptures which we so admire in his works. Prayer, the recitation of the Psalms, and study strengthened his heart and preserved him from daydreaming, sadness, and boredom. Although he was strictly forbidden to receive the sacraments, even the Eucharist, divine grace flooded his soul during these hours of prayer.

The arguments and tenderness of his sisters were ineffective against a mind so well trained in dialectic and a heart so thoroughly imbued with divine teachings. Thomas spoke freely with them. He spoke to them of God, of prayer, and of the excellence of religious life. Some years later, he was to persuade his sister, Marotta, to enter the monastery of the Benedictines of Capua, where she would become abbess. Historians have been deeply interested in this vocation. We must remember that the conversion was relative. Marotta could continue to encourage Thomas to follow her example, to enter the Benedictine Order. No one was asking any more of him. Certainly Marotta did not have to submit to the cruel opposition of her mother and family. But neither did she become the great saint or reformer as did St. Colette and St. Theresa of Avila.

When his brothers returned from their expedition with the army, the surveillance and vexations were redoubled. His Dominican habit was torn off. His sisters were given the task of offering him the Benedictine habit or student's robe in exchange. Thomas was determined to wear the holy clothes that he had humbly requested from God, from the Virgin, and from St. Dominic. The cavaliers, Reginald and Landulf, were apprenticed to another kind of existence. They were subject to the temptations which are common in a soldier's life. Reginald was a *poet amoureux,* a singer of licentious stories. Thus the two brothers, at their mother's insistence, decided to submit Thomas, a young and handsome youth, to a test which would certainly prove more effective than the tenderness of his sisters. They brought one of their friends from Naples who was noted for her beauty, and after telling her their plan, they brought her secretly into the tower during the night.

Ever since the eighteenth century, the story has been reported how Thomas, seizing a log from the fire, put the unfortunate girl to flight, and then drew a cross on the wall to keep tempting images and memories from ever gaining access to his cell. The miracle and reward which followed upon his victory are likewise well-known. After praying that God preserve him from every impurity, Thomas went to sleep. In the depth of his sleep, two angels appeared to him and drew the ends of a glowing cord around his waist. He cried out in pain and awoke, and from that day forward he was never bothered by what St. Paul called the stings of the flesh.

William of Tocco relates this story in his testimony at the process of canonization and in his biography of Thomas. He heard it from Brother Reginald of Piperno, the disciple, confidant, and confessor of the Saint. The chronicler recorded the episode in lyric phrases: "This was the siege in which the battlements are usually razed, the Cedars of Lebanon uprooted, a struggle in which we find many champions and very few conquerors." In the mind of the biographer, the miracle of the angelic cord was a supernatural affirmation of Thomas' future freedom from temptations of the flesh. The experience of confession teaches directors that, if such temptations are fatal to young people who are less chaste or to men deprived of a moral and religious education, Christian adolescents, seminarians, and religious resist them more easily with the help of God. We are inclined to believe that this victory was probably the crowning triumph of a long series of similar battles fought by Thomas during his early life.[9]

[9]Thomas of Cantimpré wrote that, doubtlessly, several women were brought into the prison during a certain period of time; "Fratres eius cogitantes per quod possent juvenilem animum evertere, cum illo mulieres in carcere per tempus aliquod concluserunt" (*Bonum universale de apibus*, I, cap. XXII). According to Tocco, the temptation and victory took place in the tower of the Château of St. John toward the end of Thomas' detention, after his brothers had returned from their military expedition. Tolomeo of Lucca knew only of the place of imprisonment, "un certain Château appelé Saint-Jean." Without leaving the army, his brothers sent Thomas back to his mother under heavy escort, and the test of his virtue was made on their return. The cord with which he was bound is preserved today in the Convent of Chieri, in Piedmont. As a remembrance of the vision, Thomas used to gird himself with the cord. Brother Reginald took it from him when he died, and put it in the hands of the Master General, John of Vercelli. The witnesses at the process of canonization did not mention these details, and Brother Reginald of Piperno ignores them.

Such constancy of will ended by breaking the stubborn opposition of his family. For a time, the boldness of John of San Guiliano increased the surveillance. According to the testimony of Bartholomew of Capua, this priest was even captured, held for a while, and then set free. Thomas' brothers had returned to the army of Frederick II. Countess Theodora felt herself virtually conquered by the supernatural perseverance of her son as his liberation approached. It is also probable that the intervention or protests of the Master General of the Friars Preachers before the Pope and Emperor hastened Thomas' release. John of San Guiliano, in agreement with Thomas, decided to hasten the solution. One night, some of the Friars came to the tower after having stationed horses afar off. By means "of a rope," Thomas slid along the side of the wall and fell into the arms of his confessor and Religious brothers. The next morning he was already far on the way to Rome. This time Countess Theodora did not even have the energy to arrest the fugitive.[10]

[10]The escape has been made more dramatic in legend. St. Thomas, like St. Paul, is said to have been let down from the tower in a basket. The chroniclers were haunted by analogies to Scripture. Tolomeo of Lucca speaks only of a rope: "Per personas privatas (Frater Thomas) ordinavit quod fratres sui ordinis de nocte venirent ad murum castri, quia se cum fune dimitteret. Sicque factum est. Ac statim animalia sunt parata ad ipsum reducendum Romam" (op. cit., cap. XXI). Father Mandonnet admits the liberation as an historic fact, pure and simple. This opinion is confirmed

Thomas Aquinas' extraordinary perseverance rapidly became legendary in the Order. Even before his death, without giving his name, Thomas of Cantimpré and Gérard de Fachet, writing in their *Vies des Frères,* cited this constancy as an example.

Thomas had been imprisoned for a little more than a year, from May 1244 to the end of the year 1245. From now on Brother Thomas Aquinas was free, and he could wear peacefully and publicly the Dominican colors which he fought for so heroically. The trial of his vocation went on, however. Innocent IV had just imposed a year's probation on all novices. Thomas would have to wait for a year before taking vows; and from the time of vows to the reception of major orders he must have undergone many more temptations and trials.

The Master General, John the Teuton, an energetic and farsighted administrator, did not hesitate to resume the plan which had been so unfortunately thwarted a little more than a year before. Thomas

by Gérard de Frachet in his *Vies des Frères:* "Desperantes de mutatione animi ejus dimisserunt eum." Finally, a remark which could edify those who are not aware of the freedom taken by chroniclers in writing history: William of Tocco, who describes the escape in his biography, testifies, in the process of canonization, that Thomas was returned to the Order by his family: "Tandem victi parentes et fratres sui ejus constantia, restituerunt ipsum ordini" (Boll., *op. cit.,* p. 705). It is possible to reconcile all these texts by admitting that the family let Thomas escape freely.

Aquinas, who had given such exceptional proof of his intelligence at Naples, was to be sent to the most famous university of Christendom, the University of Paris.[11]

At the same time, doubtlessly at the command of the General Chapter held at Cologne, the most scholarly philosopher of his time, Albert the Great,

[11]The first biographers and the most authentic historians after them, Echard, Touron, etc., say that Thomas was brought directly to Cologne by the Master General, John the Teuton, stopping only for a short time in Paris. Tolomeo writes: "Inde (Roma) vadit Coloniam ad fratrem Albertum" (*op. cit.*, cap XXI). William of Tocco says: "Quem Frater Joannes Teutonicus . . . duxit ipsum Parisios et deinde Coloniam: ubi sub Fratre Alberto Magistro in Theologia ejusdem Ordinis florebat studium generale; qui reputabatur in omni scientia singularis" (Boll., *op. cit.*, p. 660). Thomas of Cantimpré writes: "In Coloniam Agrippinam venit, studuitque in loco illo, quousque praeclarus lector Fratrum ibidem, frater Albertus Parisios translatus est" (*de apibus*, I, cap. XX). For this reason, Echard writes: "Certum est Thomam sub Alberto Coloniae primum studuisse, idque saltem per annum" (*Scriptores Ordinis Praedicatorum*, I, p. 175). But we must point out that the early chroniclers committed important errors. Tolomeo writes mistakenly that Thomas Aquinas was twenty-five years old when he came to Paris for the first time. Tocco tells us that Thomas was sent to the *studium generale* at Cologne. But this *studium* did not exist until 1248. And despite the reputation of Albert the Great, we cannot see why Thomas would have been sent to Cologne to a simple *studium* in 1244 rather than to the University of Paris. We propose that Thomas was sent directly from Rome to Paris in 1245. Nevertheless the traditional opinion which said that he studied in Cologne for a year before the time at Paris is not totally incredible. If this were the case, however, the reception of the habit would have had to occur a year earlier, before the death of Thomas' father, which is very improbable. And consequently all the other dates would have to be adjusted also.

was assigned to the *studium generale* of the Dominicans at Paris. According to the scholastic custom, he began lecturing on the fourteenth of September. It was not long before Thomas arrived at Paris. The two greatest philosophic geniuses of the thirteenth century were working in conjunction. We must admire the outstanding administration of John the Teuton who was willing to deprive Cologne of an exceptional master and Naples of an exceptional student, in order to direct them both toward Paris. What vitality in the young body of the Order of Preachers! The stagnant life which would appear a century later was as yet unknown. This vitality was a new thing. The Religious of the ancient Orders made a vow of stability, living and dying in their monastery. But social conditions had changed, necessitating a new monastic organization. This was certainly a providential occurrence; and from a purely human point of view, what good fortune it was for a student of St. Thomas' genius to be placed under the direction of a master like Albert the Great. The hesitations, gropings, and long search were over. His docility and attention spared Thomas at least ten years of study on his own.

Thomas' attitude to the instruction of a master who was justly called "The Great" was precisely that of an extremely docile and modest disciple. Thomas Aquinas, from his twentieth to twenty-fifth year, gave all, even his superiors, an exemplary

lesson of intellectual discipline. He did not claim
imprudently to be self-taught, original, or ahead of
the times. He was passive in the best sense of the
term. Passivity of spirit, in the Thomistic sense of
the term, presupposes a certain activity, a constant
rumination, an incessant labor of assimilation and
integration. The prodigious work of assimilation and
what might be called an excess of interior reflection
necessitated a corresponding excess of recollection,
solitude, and silence. Thomas did not shine outward-
ly as he did when he was an assistant lecturer at
Naples. He purposely hid his light under a basket.
He instinctively fled from conversation and recreation. This was the only apparent peculiarity which
set him apart from the rest of the students.

His fellow students began to call him by the
scornful but nevertheless well-founded nickname,
the "Dumb Ox." The name could easily have arisen
from his outward appearance. The evidence of witnesses is unanimous in picturing Thomas as a very
big man. Taking what we know of the stature of
men in the Middle Ages, we might imagine him
as a man of about six feet three inches in height.
When he went walking with his brothers, the people
in the street would make the Sign of the Cross as
he passed by. He had the sensitive skin that he
would later say was favorable to study. This bodily
physique could easily have deceived those at Cologne into thinking that Brother Thomas was a

German. This error is explained by his maternal ancestry. On his mother's side, St. Thomas descended from the Normans, the men of the North as the name indicates. From them he inherited his athletic frame, his height, his weight, and the softness and abundance of flesh. Such a physique was as far from the Greek ideal as possible. After reading the witnesses at the process of canonization, it is impossible to reject the epithets: *magnus, grossus, brutus.* This last quality, a dark complexion, reveals the Saint's Mediterranean ancestry. He descended on his father's side from the Lombards; from this race he inherited his coloring. We see that the Saint was extremely, astonishingly, sensitive. His brothers and disciples were shocked by this quality (*miro modo passibilis*). His Italian and almost feminine delicateness contributed to a fineness, a quickness of feeling, and intelligence. This alliance, this joining of the powerful Norman qualities with the delicate Lombard traits, produced, even physically, a man of both extraordinary strength and fineness. His nickname, the "Dumb Ox of Sicily," was therefore only a half-truth.

Contrary to what is implied in the legend, we do not believe that St. Albert the Great was slow to recognize the value of Brother Thomas, who had been so highly recommended to him. The dominant quality of the Master was penetration of character, the gift of observation. Moreover, the big, silent student was visible and remarkable enough that St. Albert would have taken a special interest in him. It is quite feasible and even certain that most of the students at Paris and Cologne were mistaken about the worth of the young man who worked so silently and profoundly, never wanting to be distracted from his task.

In 1248, the *studium generale* of Paris had become too large. It comprised four hundred students. Four other convents of study were created, the most important of which was at Cologne. Albert the Great had been assigned as Regent of the school; he took Thomas with him, which indicates that he realized the young student's potentialities.

William of Tocco relates at length the episode which he entitled "the revelation of the genius of St. Thomas Aquinas." At least the essentials seem to be authentic. St. Albert the Great interpreted the tract on *The Divine Names*. Brother Thomas, who was about twenty-five years old, had become the Master's collaborator. He was no longer a schoolboy nor a student of the second or third year as the legend intimates. At this time he was certainly capable of answering St. Albert's objections, and able to uphold his side in a public debate with the Master. The students did not suspect Thomas' genius. They continued to call him the "Dumb Ox." The Master, feeling that the time had come to dispel their doubts, began a public discussion in which he debated against Brother Thomas, forcing him to his final strongholds by more and more concise arguments. But at the moment when the students, silent in their admiration, thought that Thomas was surrounded, he escaped by a fine distinction which cut short all difficulty. "You solved the problem more like a doctor than a disciple," said St. Albert. Thomas finally answered: "Master, there was nothing else I could do."[12]

[12]The chroniclers of the thirteenth century were great story tellers. It is important to distinguish in their works the real from the symbolic, without excluding one or the other. Here is a condensed translation of William of Tocco's account: "In the *studium* of Cologne, Brother Thomas became so quiet that the students began to call him the 'Dumb Ox,' not knowing that he would become a master of doctrine. When St. Albert began to interpret the book of the *Divine Names* of Dionysius, Thomas listened with more attention than ever. A student, thinking that Thomas could not understand anything of it, offered charitably to repeat the lesson. Accepting humbly, Thomas thanked him. Later, this same student became confused in his explanation. Thomas, understanding the wishes of God, exposed the whole question, adding considerations which the Master had not covered. After that the tutor became the disciple. But from a scruple of conscience, and although Thomas had forbidden him to, the student went to Albert with his discovery. About that time it happened that St. Albert was exposing a very difficult question which Thomas reduced to a single page. Another brother found it lying by his door and brought it to Albert, who asked the Master of Students to have Thomas prepare to answer the question on the following day. Thomas prepared by study and prayer. The next day he upheld his thesis in public, repeated and resolved all the objections which were given to him. Albert judged the moment had come for him to intervene personally, and he presented in order four difficulties which were

During the same year, the student commented on St. Albert's course on the Divine Names. His notes on it still remain (we possess the writings of St. Thomas from his twenty-fifth year). He was not a calligrapher: his thought was too quick for his hand to follow. The writing is thick and insufficiently articulated. A little later, he commented on the Master's course on Aristotle's *Ethics*.

About the time that Brother Thomas was to receive major orders, the subdiaconate, diaconate, and the priesthood, his family renewed their attempt to dissuade him from his vocation. His uncle and brothers had incurred Frederick II's wrath by siding with the Pope against the irascible tyrant. Reginald, Thomas' own brother, had been executed. The château of Aquino with all of its dependencies was sacked and pillaged. The Emperor died shortly afterwards in 1250. Thomas' mother, sisters, and relatives begged him to accept the dignity of Abbot of Monte Cassino. By this change, he could contribute more effectively than anyone else to return the lost fortune of the family. Knowing his attachment to the Dominican habit, they had even obtained permission from Innocent IV to allow him

worthy of a famous master. Everyone thought that Thomas was cornered. But he placed a distinction which finished the debate. 'You defined like a master,' said St. Albert. Then prophetically inspired, he added: 'We call him a *Dumb Ox,* but by his doctrine, his bellowing will be heard around the world . . .'" (see Boll., *op. cit.,* p. 661).

to keep the habit as Abbot of the Benedictine monastery.[13]

What reasons could have appeared graver or more sufficient to counsel acceptance than the plight of his widowed mother suffering from the loss of a murdered son, the ruin of the family domain, and the offer of Pope Innocent IV? Moreover, Thomas could keep the habit and still be a Dominican. Who would have found it hard to accept the office? What director would not have allowed him, and even counseled him, to accept? Who knew at this time that Thomas Aquinas would become a light of the Church? If the Saint refused to be named Abbot of Monte Cassino to help his family and to console his mother, he surely must have had a very clear knowledge of the particular vocation, the mission God had called him to fulfill. Enlightened by grace, he refused.

Disheartened by his refusal, his mother and the whole family tried the one final course open to

[13]Tolomeo of Lucca writes that the position of Abbot of Monte Cassino was offered to him while he was still at Cologne: "Ibidem existens (Coloniae) oblata fuit eidem abbatia Montis Cassini per Alexandrum gratia parentum, qui jam erant expulsi de regno, et recusavit." The fact appears to be true, but Tolomeo mistakenly wrote *Alexander* for Innocent, which has led many historians into error. If this offer took place when Thomas was in Cologne, the Pope in question could only have been Innocent IV. William of Tocco attributed the offer to Clement IV (See Boll., *op. cit.*, p. 671). It is very possible that the archiepiscopacy had been offered to Thomas many times. But Tocco must have been mistaken here as he is in so many other places.

them. They succeeded in getting the Pope to offer him the archiepiscopacy of Naples with the rich revenues of the Abbey of St. Peter attached to it. If Thomas nourished the least ambition, the least desire for greatness, what more could he hope for than to become the Archbishop of Naples before his thirtieth year? Endowed with knowledge, eloquence, genius, and a commanding appearance, belonging to one of the seven most noble families of Italy, he could hope someday to become a cardinal and even more. It would be a source of wealth and honor for his family.

We would be mistaken about the habits of Religious if we thought that Thomas Aquinas did not speak frequently to St. Albert about the needs of society and the Church. The Master had shown him the great work to be done. Christian doctrine, dogma and moral, was threatened; it ran the risk of being submerged by the invasion of Aristotelianism from Greece and Spain. Christian theology and philosophy had to assimilate and absorb this wide and deep current of Peripateticism. The task appeared formidable to say the least. Albert the Great had been the first to recognize and to undertake this great work. Like the prophet he was, Albert discerned that Brother Thomas was the doctor, the saint predestined to finish the task he had himself begun. Albert advised Thomas to devote himself to this mission. And Thomas, faithful to God's grace, refused both the Abbot's chair at Monte Cassino and the episcopacy of Naples. He would be a Friar Preacher in every sense of the term.

When speaking of the vocation of Thomas Aquinas, we must be very sure to make no mistake about our point of departure. Leaving the world with its licit and illicit joys and pleasures was quite a different thing for Thomas than it was for other saints like Augustine or even St. Bernard. Thomas had scarcely known these joys. He had hardly experienced them. The beginning of his vocation was the Benedictine life. He might be said to have been born a Benedictine.

The culmination of the call was the Dominican life lived in the full rigor of the thirteenth century. The model Friar Preacher, living his vocation completely and in an outstanding manner, was essentially a doctor and master. Thomas felt that this was his vocation.

Social and religious evolution had created a wide gap between the concept of a Benedictine or Cistercian monk at the end of the twelfth century and the Dominican monk in the middle of the thirteenth century. The Benedictines were an ancient Order. The Dominicans were modern. St. Thomas was born to a feudal family, and vowed at the age of reason to the Benedictine discipline. At eighteen he attempted an act of individual liberty. The son of an important and influential Medieval lord left the rich feudal monastery, situated like a fortified castle on the summit of a hill, where the abbot was a noble and absolute monarch. He became a Mendicant Religious, living in a common house in the most populous quarter of the city. Instead of overseeing the colonization and cultivation of vast domains, he wished to devote his life to teaching Aristotelian dialectic, philosophy, Scripture, and theology in a poor classroom of the convent. Thomas' vocation is an example of the evolution, the new world, the new epoch of civilization.

It is not surprising that, in winning his vocation, in the transition from the Benedictine life, to which he had been vowed as a child, to the Dominican life he freely chose, Thomas had to overcome the opposition caused by all the prejudices of his class: the excess of family authority, armed violence, brutal temptations against his virtue, and the seduction of honors and benefices offered to the young noble priest. Every abuse of feudal civilization can be found in the means taken to avert from his destiny the man who was to become one of the most famous figures of the Universal Church.

We can say without exaggeration that Thomas Aquinas' vocation, from its point of departure to its term, from the nature of all the opposition he encountered, typifies the social and religious evolution accomplished in the first half of the thirteenth century.

Two: DOCTRINE AND APOLOGY

St. Thomas was the disciple of St. Albert for about seven years. He first studied under him at Paris, then at Cologne. When he was twenty-five years old (c. 1250), shortly after his ordination, Thomas was appointed assistant to the Master, working and teaching under Albert's direction. His penetrating intellect, his excellent memory, his endless and prodigious labor, and finally his genius soon approached the excellence of Albert. Although he would never attain the infinite and almost excessive scholarship of his Master, Thomas had already gained depth, precision, and clarity of thought.

Judging from the practice of medieval schools, Thomas would have first been assigned as a *cursor biblicus,* his task being to read and give a rapid commentary on the entire Bible. Such a course extended over a two-year period. It seems that, just before he left Cologne, Thomas had already been asked to comment on the *Sentences* of Peter Lombard.

He performed these tasks so brilliantly that Albert was led to make a decision which earned him the title, "Great." Discarding all personal interest, Albert chose to be separated from his favorite disciple in order to elevate him to the first place by assigning him to the University of Paris.

In this advancement of Thomas, Albert was thinking of the progress of civilization and of Christianity. It was of primary importance that the renewed Aristotelian method, which he himself had begun, be represented at the University of Paris by a worthy spokesman. Since it was also necessary to introduce the Aristotelian doctrine into Germany, Master Albert could not leave Cologne. The task of defending and propagating this new method at Paris was assigned to Thomas, for he alone was capable of doing it.

Albert's proposal probably appeared as an illusion or dream to others. He was suggesting that Thomas, who was only about twenty-seven years old, be assigned to the convent of Saint-Jacques as a *Bachelarius Sententiarum* slated to become a Master of Theology. No one could be promoted to this degree until he was at least thirty-five years old. Since there were many competitors for the master's chair already living at Saint-Jacques, the nomination of Thomas Aquinas must have appeared to be a shocking injustice. Despite the fact that the Master General had personally protected the young student, Albert's proposal seemed impossible to him.

The Regent of Cologne had no concept of protocol; he lived in a world of ideas. John the Teuton, an energetic and rigorous superior, answered with a categorical denial.

Like John the Teuton, Albert was German; he was as opinionated as the Master General, but more flexible. His small stature, slight build, extreme refinement, and courtesy surprised those who met him. He numbered many influential people among his friends, one of whom was the famous Dominican Cardinal, Hugh of Saint-Cher, who is noted for his critical works on Holy Scripture.

Hugh was passing through Cologne at the time, and Albert presented the whole matter to him. He stressed Thomas' extraordinary competence and the need for him at Paris. The Cardinal, who had been a professor at the University of Paris, a prior of the convent of Saint-Jacques, and Provincial of France, sided with Albert. He intervened with all his influence, and it was not long before Thomas received his assignment to Saint-Jacques. He left for Paris immediately to begin teaching when classes reconvened in September, 1252.

The ease and strength which Thomas showed on the way from Cologne to Paris foreshadowed the spirit of his life's work. This was certainly an indication to the Dominicans of Thomas' vocation. But it is also remarkable that the Order was so unhesitating and straightforward in directing Thomas to a scientific career. His superior intelligence and genius were allowed free development by the members of his Dominican family. Even in Religious Orders this is so rare an occurrence that it demands particular mention.

In the middle of his twenty-seventh year, Thomas Aquinas taught his first class in the same lecture hall where he had been a student only a few years earlier. We do not know whether he was a *Bachelarius Biblicus*. The biographers mention only his success as a *Bachelarius Sententiarum*. We know that he had taken Albert's course at Cologne, and that probably he had already begun to interpret the *Sentences* of Peter Lombard. We still possess his *Commentary* on the four books of the *Sentences,* which constitutes his first masterpiece. The echo of his teaching resounded throughout Paris. As Albert had predicted, the "bellowing" of his doctrine began to attract both disciples and enemies in large numbers.

Thomas Aquinas certainly appeared to his contemporaries as an innovator, a young professor who was renewing theology from top to bottom. Even in the process of his canonization and in the works of his first biographer, William of Tocco, who was concerned mostly with his ascetic and mystical virtues, the echo of astonishment caused by the newness of his doctrine is recorded in rich and meaningful expressions. A passage of the biographer on the subject has become famous. Although the repetition of the term *novus* is almost impossible to render in English, we have attempted to translate it as literally as possible.

> After St. Thomas had become a *bachelarius,* he began to expose in this teaching the reflections which, during the time of his silent study, he had accumulated in his mind. God truly poured knowledge into him. Indeed, teaching flowed from his lips in such a god-like way that he seemed to surpass everyone, including the full professors. Moreover, by the lucid quality of his teaching he was better able than others to stimulate the students to a love of learning. He raised new issues in his lectures, finding new and clearer ways of proving points and turning arguments into proofs. Anyone who heard him teach these new things and settle doubtful matters with new arguments could not help but wonder whether God had not enlightened him with rays of a new light, especially since he immediately began to be so steady in judgment that he did not hesitate to teach and write new views with which God might deign to inspire him in new ways.[1]

In this matter, history confirms the testimony of the witnesses and biographers on every score. How-

[1]Bollandists, *Acta Sanctorum* (VII Mars), I, p. 661. William of Tocco, defending his Master, insinuates the nature of this novelty. "It should not appear absurd to many that, in sacred doctrine, someone should make use of the science of his day." This secular science was philosophy; and it was philosophy which renewed the theological teaching given by Thomas.

ever little one is aware of the ideological movements of the thirteenth century, a reading of the first question, or even the first article, of the *Commentary on the Sentences* would suffice to present the essential character of the novelty presented in the teaching of St. Thomas. Peter Lombard's text is obviously relegated to second place. What is important are the new articles introduced in the commentary, the new way of precising and ordering them, and the new philosophical reason brought to bear on the argumentation. St. Augustine is still quoted frequently, but less often than Aristotle. This is the key figure: Aristotle. Thomas proceeds according to the principles of Aristotelian methodology: potency, act, categories, etc. Generally, he uses the mold of peripatetic metaphysics and ethics, pouring into it the content of theology. Or, on the contrary, he enlarges the Aristotelian theses, goes beyond their narrow limits, and adapts their too simple structure to Christian revelation. To be exact, Thomas had undertaken a recasting of both Peripateticism and the teaching of theology.

As we have just said, the first article of the *Commentary on the Sentences* alone suffices to indicate the new method employed. This article is worthy of the *Summa*. It can hardly be doubted that Brother Thomas began his courses with the solution to the stated problem. From the first, he went to the root of the difficulties disturbing his times, solving them clearly.[2]

In the first article of this *Commentary*, Thomas establishes the distinction between philosophy and theology. He indicates the proper limit and method of each. Theology is based on premises drawn from revealed truths, philosophy on premises known through natural reason. However these two sciences are related to one another, philosophy serves theology. This "distinction without separation" of the two sciences permitted Thomas to use the principles, rules, and framework of Aristotelian philosophy to build his monumental work on a solid foundation. Later on in this book, we shall investigate his philosophical and theological synthesis.

Did the new method imply a rash boldness on the part of the young professor? There is no doubt about it. First of all, the widespread revival of Aristotle's teaching since the beginning of the thirteenth century had been formally condemned by the Church. The mere use of the Peripatetic method was suspect of heresy (*sapit heresim*) by the whole school of theology which might be called Augustinian or traditionalist in the true sense of the word.

[2]We can quickly grasp the qualities of the new Albertino-Thomistic method by comparing Article One of the first question of Thomas' *Commentary on the Sentences* with Question III of the Prologue or *Proemium* of St. Bonaventure's commentary on the same work. St. Bonaventure holds that theology is an "affective science." He was writing a poetical work for edification. The *Commentary* of St. Thomas is rigorously scientific.

The introduction of Peripatetic or Aristotelian philosophy into the West, into the Latin and Christian world, caused a veritable crisis among men of letters. At the time of Abelard, the *Organon* (Aristotle's dialectical and logical tracts) raised questions about the universal which upset less firmly rooted beliefs. In the thirteenth century, when all the books of Aristotle, including his ethics, metaphysics, and psychology entered Europe through Spain, the danger became acute. The dangerous teaching of Peripateticism arrived in the Latin West along with the interpretation of the commentator Averroes. It is important to note that Peripateticism and Averroism at the time of Albert the Great and St. Thomas were considered as one. But Averroistic Peripateticism combined with its excellent qualities formidable errors, destructive of religion and even of natural morality.

It is true that Peripateticism, because of the power of its synthesis, the depth of its principles, and the rigor of its deductions, appeared as the work of a genius, as a brilliant revelation. According to Avicenna, Aristotle should rather be venerated as a god and a messiah than consulted as a man. Nevertheless this new philosophy taught that the souls of men were mortal, that the world existed from all time without beginning, that God created out of necessity, that Providence, properly so-called, is a pious opinion, that fatalism or determinism rules our actions. Consequently, merit, punishment, and eternal recompense are popular illusions. Religions were considered as poetic and symbolic mythology, which the wise could respect, but really ought to abandon. Since these principles were interconnected and followed on the first principles which supported the whole system, it seemed impossible to take hold of one cog without being fatally dragged in and crushed by the whole system.

Charged to defend the souls of the faithful against the enchantment of new and pernicious teachings, the Church did not fail in her task. When she sees cities and the countryside suddenly threatened by some new flood of evil, the first measure taken is to set up as high and solid a defense as possible. The second step is to try to prevent a flood by a thousand drainage canals which, far from devastating the land, fertilize it. The first means of protection was employed by the Church in 1210, when the Provincial Council of Sens prohibited, under pain of excommunication, the interpretation of the philosophical works of Aristotle. In 1215, the papal Legate, Robert of Courson, confirmed this prohibition. For a while these excommunications kept Peripateticism at the periphery of Christianity. However, Gregory IX, the nephew of Innocent III, one of the most energetic promoters of science in Christendom, quickly recognized that the rigorous prohibition of the books of Aristotle was a violent measure which could have only temporary success. He took the initiative to use the second means of defense, the only definitive and worthwhile one: the assimilation and absorption of Peripateticism by Christianity. On April 13, 1231, he ordered that the University of Paris observe the prohibition of the works of Aristotle until they could be thoroughly examined by three masters whom he appointed to the task.

Catholic and non-Catholic historians alike have praised the initiative of this Pontiff. Unfortunately, the three Masters of the University could not accomplish the task demanded of them. They were neither capable of it nor did they have the necessary materials. For a good beginning, they needed the authentic text of Aristotle, a literal translation of the Greek, and a perfect knowledge of Scripture, of the Fathers of the Church, and of Christian doctrine. This was one of those critical times in history, when an enormous task arises which only a genius can recognize and undertake. The Order of Preachers would later assume the responsibility of assimilating and absorbing Aristotelian philosophy into Christian tradition. During the interim, however, the Church's prohibition of the books remained in force.

Although the excommunication could be leveled only against the Masters who commented on the books of Aristotle, and not against those who made passing reference to him, anyone who cited the Peripatetic too frequently was certainly frowned upon by the theologians, or more precisely by the proponents of the traditionalist method. Even in the Order of Preachers there was opposition to the use of natural philosophy in the teaching of theology. The Constitutions of 1228 are categorical on this point: "Let the Brothers not study the books of profane authors and philosophers." This prohibition was repeated from the interdictions of 1210 and 1215. In 1228, Pope Gregory IX reproached certain Masters of the University of Paris for "speaking the language of philosophers" in their courses, that is, for quoting them as authorities too frequently. In 1230, John of Saint-Giles, the first Master of the second chair at the convent of Saint-Jacques, condemned certain doctors for failing to detach themselves from Aristotle in their study of theology. They were "exchanging gold for copper by introducing philosophical questions into sacred doctrine." The generation of Dominicans who were maturing around the year 1231, at the time of the prohibitions, would generally remain hostile to the introduction of the Aristotelian method into theology. St. Albert the Great, in a moment of impatience, wrote to them: "There are people who know nothing and who wish to fight in every way they can the use of philosophy. They are especially strong among the Preachers where there is no one to resist them; stupid beings (*bruta animalia*) who blaspheme what they do not understand."[3] It goes without saying that the Franciscan doctors remained faithful to the Augustinian tradition, and were even more opposed than the Dominicans to those who attempted to adopt Peripateticism.

Albert the Great, whose own teaching had obtained an unheard-of success, prepared the way as a sort of precursor for Thomas Aquinas. The young doctor would need much initiative, patience, daring, and prudence to bring his task to a successful conclusion. A new obstacle, which Albert had not faced, was developing at Paris, where the secular masters were waging a battle against the teaching of the newly-founded Religious Orders.

Although the campaign was directed against the Religious Orders in general, the Dominicans and especially the two Regents of the convent of Saint-Jacques were most especially under attack. The Friars Preachers, who were required to study by their founder, St. Dominic, were dispensed by law from choral office and observances when they taught. Incorporated into the University of Paris from their

[3]We do not wish to multiply references in a work designed for popular reading. Documentation can be found in the *Chartularium Universitatis Parisiensis*, published by Denifle and Chatelain, and in the important work of P. Mandonnet, *Siger de Brabant*. For information about the Dominican milieu, it is necessary to read the excellent works of P. Mortier, *Histoire des Maîtres Généraux de l'Ordre des Frères Prêcheurs*, especially the first two volumes.

very beginnings, they were growing so rapidly that they had become formidable competitors of the secular masters.

We must not think of the University of Paris in terms of the monumental edifice of the actual Sorbonne, as comprising a single institution. The University was still only a loosely-organized association of schools or doctoral chairs. The Franciscans had the right to one chair, and taught in their convent. The Dominicans had the right to two chairs, and taught in the two large lecture halls adjoining Saint-Jacques. The secular masters did the same or joined with one another. The Canons of Notre-Dame taught in the cloister of the Cathedral. The masters did not comment on separate matter, one on dogma, another on ethics, another on the New Testament. No differentiation or organization of the courses was in effect. While Thomas was interpreting, or rather commenting on, the *Sentences,* Bonaventure or John Peckham commented in his convent, and William of Saint-Amour or some other secular master commented on them at the same time in another section of the city. Everything converged to bring the situation into open conflict.

Many advantages were offered to the students and professors of a great convent such as that of Saint-Jacques, with its adjoining church, lecture halls, common life, mutual assistance, constant application to intensive study, and the presence of outstanding masters, geniuses like Albert the Great and

Thomas Aquinas. The situation of the seculars was in great peril. The convent of Saint-Jacques, and not what would later be the college of Robert of Sorbonne, had to a great extent become the center of the University.

The secular masters saw their danger clearly. They battled with all their strength against any encroachment by the Preachers. Hostilities were declared the very year Thomas Aquinas began his teaching. In February, 1252, the secular masters of the University gathered privately, and published a decree prohibiting the religious from holding more than one chair at the University. This article was obviously aimed at the Preachers, for they alone held two chairs. What authority was denying them their acquired right? They refused to obey the prohibition of the secular masters. A few months after the decree, Thomas took one of the two chairs in question. The brilliance of his teaching attracted a great number of students, overshadowing still more the diminishing popularity of the seculars. Thomas' success certainly added to their zeal. Still only a *Bachelarius*, he was attacked personally, although indirectly, by his adversaries. We need only to call to mind the decrees which barred religious from access to the masterate. In April of 1253, an ordinance was published which prohibited any professor holding the Baccalaureate or Licentiate from becoming a master unless he swore to submit to the decisions promulgated by the body of the University. Naturally the Dominicans could not subject themselves to this requirement, since they would be forced to discontinue one of their own chairs of theology, the one where Thomas was sending forth his rays of light and truth.

It was not long before hostilities turned into public injuries and even assault. The two Regents of Saint-Jacques were expelled from the University, and a prohibition was placed on students attending their classes or those of their assistants, which consequently included St. Thomas. The Friars were attacked in the streets. The deans of the University entered the lecture hall of Saint-Jacques and attempted to read the sentence of excommunication. They were quickly shown the door by the student brothers. Humbert of the Romans relates in a letter that the Preachers were beaten up and spat upon, and that the people threw straw and other "disagreeable and dangerous" objects at them. Despite his height, it would have been dangerous for Thomas to go out of the priory alone at night. Such an acute state of crisis could only be cleared up by intervention from Rome. Pope Innocent IV called four masters of the University to the Curia.

It has been said that, although William of Saint-Amour was born "Saint-Amour," he was a man with a heart full of hate. We might add the qualities of violence and sedition besides. He went to Rome and succeeded in winning several influential prelates to his side, so as to be heard favorably by Innocent IV, whose position soon changed. The quarrel between the Religious and the seculars was not limited merely to the question of university teachings. Parish priests complained bitterly of seeing their flocks desert their churches and confessionals for those of the Preachers and Friars Minor, giving up their bodies, souls, and possessions. The faithful man delivered his soul by his confidence, his goods in donations and estates, and his body by having it interred in the cemeteries of the Mendicants. William of Saint-Amour confused the two questions of teaching and ministry, and presented to Innocent IV the partially real abuses committed by certain Religious. During the year 1254, pontifical decrees sliced away at the privileges of the Friars. According to Thomas of Cantimpré, the whole Roman Curia was against the Friars Preachers. William of Saint-Amour had won their support. In June and July, bulls favoring the cause of the University submitted the Regents of Saint-Jacques to its decrees, thus attacking Thomas Aquinas almost directly. It would be interesting to know what his reaction was when this sudden calamity struck the Order and the convent of Saint-Jacques. He prayed with the brothers and recited the Litanies of the Saints. Given his character, it is probable that he remained the calmest among the religious. Finally, on November 12, 1254, the last decree, which appeared as the *coup de grâce,* seemed to destroy all hope, as if not only the branches but even the trunk of St. Dominic's tree was imperiled. In the bull, *Etsi animarum*, the rights and privileges of the Friars were reduced to practically nothing. Apparently the life of the Order could no longer sustain itself. Taken together and viewed in the light of previous privileges, the bulls which appeared between May and December of 1254 can only be interpreted as the most astonishing reversal in monastic and religious history.

Several reasons have been ascribed to Pope Innocent's sudden change of policy. According to Taegio, the Preachers of Genoa had refused to turn over to the Pope a plot of land which belonged to them. It seems to us that there is a broader explanation for the turn of events. The mere fact of the rather prodigious development of the Mendicant Orders, which spread over the whole of Europe in thirty years, could easily lead to a dangerous instability in the Church, similar to the danger of capsizing a ship by a sudden and notable transfer of weight. Even today, if a congregation were to multiply in quality and quantity as the Franciscans and Dominicans did between 1220 and 1250, even though no abuses were committed by its members, certain disturbances and lack of balance would necessarily result. The parish priests had a legitimate complaint that their fees and influence were failing. But this does not mean that the Friars were not justified in their development which took place within the limits set by the

Church. Whenever new and strong trees develop near older ones, the older are threatened by the strength of the younger. The task of the gardener is to see that all have a place in the sun. Pope Innocent IV could very legitimately restrain the privileges of these new Religious Orders. However, it seems to us that he was extreme in abolishing them.

A month after promulgating the bull, *Etsi animarum,* Innocent IV died and Alexander IV succeeded him. A true politician and protector of study in the Church, he was particularly interested that the Friars Preachers return to their task. Innocent III, Gregory IX, and Alexander IV contributed more effectively than anyone to intellectual civilization in the first half of the thirteenth century. The day after his election, Alexander IV annulled the bull of Innocent IV, a second and even quicker reversal than the first. We can hardly imagine the joy of the Preachers at the convent of Saint-Jacques, or the desolation of the secular masters and William of Saint-Amour. Some months later, in April of 1255, the bull, *Quasi lignum vitae,* restored the privileges of the Mendicant Orders.

The Pope pointed out the legitimate complaints of the secular clergy to the Dominican Master General, Humbert of the Romans. When he and his definitors met in council at Milan, they agreed to limit the privileges of the Order considerably, arriving at what was, or at least tended to be, a state of equilibrium. The secular masters of the University made as few concessions as possible to restore what was to be only a temporary peace. When a gambler has not won an entire sum, he finds it very difficult to hold on to his partial gain. Usually he will risk all he has and end up losing it all. William of Saint-Amour, who first had won a complete and decisive victory, resigned himself never to accept a *modus vivendi,* and so insisted on his ruin.

During these many troubles and reversals, Thomas Aquinas, impassible, continued his course and commentary on the *Sentences.* His fame was such that he soon gained the reputation of being the most representative theologian of the Order of Preachers. A very significant and important letter of the Pope proves this. The University's chancellor had decided to confer some theological degrees on the Religious. Thomas, being the first named, was theoretically already received. Alexander IV wrote his approval to the chancellor, insisting at the same time that Thomas be permitted to give his first lesson, which alone would complete the nomination.

> We have learned with true consolation that you have conferred the degree on Brother Thomas Aquinas of the Order of Preachers, a man of very high nobility, remarkable for the holiness of his character, and endowed by the grace of God with a treasure of knowledge. But, in order that the nomination be fully carried out, we ask and we command that you hold the first solemn lesson immediately.

This time it was not just the Order of Preachers,

but the Church in the person of the Pope who demanded the promotion of Thomas Aquinas. He noted Thomas' distinctive characteristics in three words: his great nobility, his virtue, and his knowledge. We are of the opinion that Alexander IV was aware that the theological teaching of Albert and Thomas bore a distinctively Aristotelian character. Had this new method been suspect in the court of Rome, the Pope would never have praised Brother Thomas in this way; nor would he have demanded his acceptance by the University so forcefully. Thomas Aquinas was the most prominent of theologians; and what is more, he had the support of the Pope and the Roman Curia.

Doubtlessly the chancellor of the University allowed Thomas to operate under his license, but William of Saint-Amour and the other secular masters opposed him with all their power, doing all they could to place insuperable obstacles in the way of the reception and advancement of the young professor.

For more than a year after his return from Rome, William of Saint-Amour continued his defense of the seculars in letters, especially a pamphlet written against the new Religious Mendicants, in which he grossly exaggerated all the major accusations and abuses. He severely criticized the innovations and denounced the new Orders, especially the Dominicans, as a danger to the Church and society. The accusatory pamphlet circulated secretly under the title, *De novissimorum temporum periculis.* The term *novissimus* has no equivalant in English, but should be understood as meaning both the modern, most recent times, and the last days, the days closest to the end of the world.

Our age has lost the preoccupation, so common among our ancestors, of judging and interpreting precursory signs. We find it difficult to understand how, not only the common person, but even Masters of Theology foretold a more or less imminent coming of the Last Judgment. William of Saint-Amour believed in good faith in the precursors of the Antichrist:[4] "At the eleventh hour, 1255 years have already passed." He probably meant that the last hour of the world had come. Jesus, and after him John and Paul, predicted that false shepherds would arise in great numbers, feigning sanctity, penetrating the cities and houses: "always learning, never reaching true wisdom." These false apostles were obviously the Preachers, a fact which William of Saint-Amour demonstrated by arguments likely to influence and rally the whole of the secular party to his cause.

Without official approval of his Order, a Franciscan of the mystical school published an important work contradicting the fundamental assertions contained in the tract *De novissimorum temporum*

[4]Even after his condemnation and exile from the university, William of Saint-Amour continued to prophesy about the Antichrist and his ministers. It was during this period that he wrote the *Liber de Antichristo et eiusdem ministris.*

periculis. The teachings of Brother Gerard were
reassuring. According to him, the world was still
far from "the last times." His work was a kind of
summa, consisting of a long preface, *Liber introduc-
torius,* and three books borrowed from the Abbot
Joachim of Flora. Two of these books were entitled
Apocalypsis nova and *Psalterium decem chordarum.*
Brother Gerard interpreted the three ages of the
world: the first age, represented by the Old Testament, was especially the age of the Father; the
second, represented by the New Testament, was
the age of the Son; the third, beginning in 1260,
would be represented by the *Evangelium Aeternum,*
that is, by the writings of Abbot Joachim, and it
would be the age of the Holy Spirit. Christianity
had just arrived at the dawn of the third age. Thus
the calculations of William of Saint-Amour were
wrong, and the spiritual and brotherly Mendicant
Religious, far from being the apostles of the Antichrist, were the special precursors of the Holy
Spirit. Brother Gerard correctly asserted the advent
of a new era, but he was mistaken about the nature
of the innovation. Soon Thomas was to reveal to
Brother Gerard and William of Saint-Amour that
the renewal consisted in the application of formal
reason in theology and mysticism.

As is the case with publications of this type,
De novissimorum temporum periculis enjoyed wide
success. Copies multiplied and were even sold in
Rome. At first they were hidden under the heavy

mantles of the Canons; but later they could be found scattered on chairs and tables of the schools. Students thought it much more interesting to argue about the Friars than to read and to criticize their manuscripts. William of Saint-Amour still numbered a few devoted disciples at Rome, who persuaded Pope Alexander IV to initiate a public examination of the question. He appointed a commission of four cardinals, and told the Masters General of the Preachers and Friars Minor to send some of their most outstanding theologians to plead their cause at Rome. A number of Religious, reminded of the reversal of Innocent IV, began to fear another attack. Like Innocent, Alexander began his reign being favorable to the Order. Perhaps he had also been persuaded to remove his favor from the Order. Humbert of the Romans quickly summoned Albert the Great and Thomas Aquinas to Rome.

How different these two men were: Albert, small, delicate, and extremely lively; Thomas Aquinas, thirty years old, in the prime of life, tall, strong, very calm, with a slow and magnanimous gait. His nobility, his serene and commanding appearance reassured the frightened Religious. He was the hope of the Order. In the presence of the Fathers assembled at the Chapter of Anagni, Humbert of the Romans left his stall, and amid general approval, placed the feared manuscript, *De novissimorum temporum periculis,* in the hands of Brother Thomas Aquinas, who was to take up the challenge, to be the *pugil fidei,* the herald of the faith for his brothers. The next day he announced to the religious: "My Fathers, I have read this book, which is full of perfidious accusations. But on examining it further, I see that it is built on sand, not on the principles of faith and the authority of the Doctors of the Church. I will refute it." Pope Alexander IV personally advised and commanded Humbert of the Romans to give the task to Thomas.

A few days later, Thomas brought in his refutation: *Contra impugnantes Dei cultum et religionem.* The *opusculum* was read publicly, and judged to be complete, exact, and apodictic. The scholastics of the thirteenth century developed a prodigious analytic and synthetic power from their daily exercise in dialectic discussion. They were able to retain and compose mentally every word and every letter of a tract. This ability to synthesize was most characteristic of Thomas Aquinas. The Saint could easily have composed the tract mentally in one night. It takes up one hundred and sixty pages in the Parma edition of his collected works. When the tract was delivered publicly, stenographers, trained to record the highly abbreviated Latin of the times, wrote down the words of the speaker. Two or three days later, the work was ready to be distributed to the Religious.[5] Napoleon and Pascal

---

[5]In the following year, St. Thomas produced the final complete edition of the *opusculum* at Paris. This has survived down to us and is dated 1257.

alone in modern times seem to have possessed as great an aptitude for mental composition.

The reading of this work would be deceptive even to the majority of cultivated readers who to-day prefer a flowing or literary discourse. Our lazy imaginations and memories are incapable of picturing or retaining even ten or twelve objections. We regret that Thomas did not write an apology for his Order in the good Latin which Erasmus might have admired. But that was not the fashion of the time. Besides, the methodological rigor would have been sacrificed. The tract was published for the members of the Chapter at Anagni and for the cardinals as an aid to their memory. All the accusations of William of Saint-Amour against the Mendicants and especially against the Friars Preachers were refuted with order and concision. The *opusculum* is clear and precise, a repertory of sources, arguments, Patristic and scriptural texts. Nothing is easier than finding the answer to a given objection.

If, for example, we wanted to find out what Thomas thought about mystical considerations and eschatological calculations concerning the last days or the various ages of the world, we would find it clearly stated in this work. The answer is peremptory, destroying the mystagogical efforts expended in false scriptural exegesis.

Those who claim that they can prove from scriptural texts that the Antichrist will come in seven or one hundred or a thousand years are the most presumptuous of men (*inveniuntur praesumptuosissimi*); for it has been written, *Non est vestrum nosse tempora vel momenta.* ("It is not for you to know the time or the moment").

The solution to other questions proved more difficult. It is true that the Mendicant Orders were new and modern. They broke from monastic tradition in order to answer the needs of their time. In the third and fourth Councils of the Lateran, the prelates, bishops, and cardinals denounced the failure of the secular clergy to preach and to teach doctrine. Priests and even bishops were poorly trained, unable to uphold their position in debate with the leaders of heresy. It was at that time that St. Dominic, encouraged by Innocent III and Honorius III, founded the Order of Preachers. The new goals they pursued were teaching in schools of higher learning and preaching dogma. This break with monastic custom necessitated corresponding modifications in the whole economy of religious discipline: the shortening of the Office and religious ceremonies; the principle of dispensation from ascetic observances; the abandonment of solitude for the populous cities; suppression of the vow of stability for a life of wandering; and the substitution of profound and constant study for manual labor.

This metamorphasis had occurred only a few

years before the time of Thomas, and consequently still appeared revolutionary. It was easy for William of Saint-Amour and his partisans to maintain that these modifications were unprecedented and even contrary to tested customs and traditions.

By answering these objections, St. Thomas explained this revolution, this evolution of monastic life. For this reason alone, the *opusculum* is of key historical value. It provides a rational and theological justification for what the Dominicans and Franciscans had done in the half-century after the deaths of their founders. But, in the mind of the secular masters of the University of Paris, even the Pope had no right to transform monastic life so essentially. Thomas established this right against the opinion of these men. It is obvious why Pope Alexander IV, the Master General of the Dominicans, and Thomas Aquinas joined together in this effort. By defending the Mendicant Orders, they justified the work of Gregory IX and Innocent III.

In such a small book we cannot repeat even the principal arguments in *Contra impugnantes*. On all the points involved, Thomas answers victoriously. He defends forcefully and with balance the dispensations, the abandoning of manual labor, collective as well as individual poverty, literary preaching, the ministry, confession, burials, the direction of families, study, and teaching in the chairs of the great Universities of Europe.[6] He deduces most of his conclusions from a general principle which should be mentioned because it can serve to remove many prejudices. Thomas says that the excellence of a Religious Order does not come from the severity of its observances, its fasts or penances, but from the excellence of the goal which it seeks. When he considers the needs of the Church which inspired the founding of his Order, in order to exemplify the final results, he waxes even more eloquent:

> Because of the ignorance of the secular priests, until this very day the decree of the Lateran Council that each metropolitan church have some doctors capable of teaching theology could not be fulfilled. But we find this decree fulfilled today by the religious, even beyond what was prescribed. Whence it appears that the prophecy of Isaiah is fulfilled that the universe is full of the knowledge of God (*repleta est terra scientia Domini*). So it is by a most salutary and opportune circumstance that a Religious Order has been instituted in which men gather to devote themselves to come to the aid of priests. And the deeds accomplished have manifested this truth as the final evidence. For we see today that, through the intervention of these religious, heretical error has been destroyed in entire regions, infidels have been

[6]The more knowledge we acquire about the thirteenth century and the Order of Preachers, the more realistic we find the abstract arguments in this *opusculum*. St. Thomas proved that a Religious could frequent the courts of princes. He defended his superior, the prior of the convent of Saint-Jacques, Nicholas of Goran, later the confessor of the King of France.

converted to the faith, the ignorant instructed in religion, and innumerable Christians entering the religious state, so that, if by a flagrant lie someone dares to hold that such a Religious Order is useless, he has obviously been persuaded to despise conversion to grace and consequently to have sinned against the Holy Ghost.[7]

This vehement attack was evidently the cry of a son defending the work of salvation performed by his religious family and their Father St. Dominic. The tract *Contra impugnantes* is thus a triumphant apology for the Mendicant Orders. Its value was recognized by the cardinals and the Pope. The defamatory pamphlet was condemned, burned in the court of Rome, and soon afterwards burned before the doctors and students of the University of Paris. William of Saint-Amour, exiled from France by St. Louis, refused to submit, and stubbornly foretold the end of the world, considering himself a persecuted prophet. Despite recurring persecution and due in great part to St. Thomas, modern Religious Orders have definitely earned their right to existence and expansion. The history of the evolution of monastic and religious life has had its high and low points. On one of the high white summits of some dangerous cliff we ought to erect a statue of Thomas Aquinas.

[7]St. Thomas Aquinas, "Contra impugnantes Dei cultum et religionem," nn. 130-131, in *Opuscula Theologica* (Rome: Marietti, 1954), pp. 30-31.

A short time after the Chapter of Anagni, probably toward the end of the summer of 1256, Brother
Thomas returned to Paris. He entered victorious.
The adversary *par excellence*, William of Saint-
Amour, was condemned in October. To complete
the victory, Alexander IV, the personal protector
of Thomas Aquinas, saw to it that he was received
immediately by the University as a Master of Theology. For a whole year, William's sympathizers at
the University waged a battle with the Holy See.
Alexander IV sent bull after bull and finally succeeded in persuading Odor of Douai and Christian of
Beauvais, personal friends of William, to promise
to receive Thomas to the Magisterate immediately.
The Pope protected the young doctor energetically.
He dispatched the document signed by the Bishop
of Paris, who threatened the Masters of the University with a declaration of perjury if they did
not confer the degree. They finally resigned themselves and placed the doctoral cap on the head of
the conqueror.

For two years Thomas held one of the two chairs
of theology at the convent of Saint-Jacques. Some-
time earlier, he had completed his *Commentary on
the Four Books of the Sentences*. Now he commented on the Gospel of St. Matthew, the tract of
Boethius on the Trinity, composed his *De veritate*,
and began the *Summa Contra Gentes*, one of the
works which would prepare him for his *Summa
Theologiae*.

Thomas undertook this *Summa Contra Gentes* on the express command of Alexander IV, who seems to have developed a partiality for the Saint. It appeared as if the Pope could not do without the young Dominican. Summoned to the papal court from 1259 to 1269, St. Thomas taught and wrote at Anagni, Orvieto, Rome, and finally at Viterbo.

This sojourn in Italy during the reigns of Alexander IV, Urban IV, and Clement IV is extremely important for two principal reasons. First of all, St. Thomas was in constant contact with the cardinals and the Pope. He became the theologian of the Curia and the Holy See. It was also during his stay in Italy that he enjoyed enough leisure to take up again, on new and more solid grounds, the study of Aristotle and the Fathers of the Church.

We have said that Pope Gregory IX prohibited the teaching of the books of Aristotle until they had been examined by competent theologians. We also pointed out that historians have praised this decision very highly. The nephew of Gregory IX and the protector of St. Thomas, Alexander IV, was fully aware of his uncle's projects and commissioned St. Albert the Great to compose a tract against the Averroists, which we possess under the title, *De unitate intellectus contra Averroem.*

The intention of the Sovereign Pontiff is evident. The Averroistic commentators had jeopardized the cause of Peripateticism by exaggerating the errors of Aristotle, especially those which tended to deny the immortality of the soul and the existence of free will. It was necessary to separate Peripateticism from the Averroistic interpretation. This was the intention which inspired the Roman Curia in the direction which it imparted to the scientific movement. At the beginning of 1256, when Thomas and Albert met at Anagni, they found the Pope and cardinals united in their determination that the errors of the Averroists be removed from the interpretation of Aristotle.

The first condition required for this task was to return directly to the source, that is, to the genuine, original Greek text. A Dominican religious, William of Moerbeke, who knew Greek perfectly, drew up a literal translation of the works of Aristotle for St. Thomas. This translation does not belong to a literary tradition, but it is scrupulously faithful. Greek scholars consider it one of the best from the viewpoint of fidelity. St. Thomas began his critical studies of these texts about the year 1263. At the same time, he returned to his literal commentaries on the principal books of the Old and New Testaments: Job, Jeremiah, Isaiah, and the four Gospels. He reread the works of the Fathers of the Church. And, gathering the most outstanding passages, he composed his famous work called the *Golden Chain (Catena Aurea)*. It was only in 1267,

toward the end of his long sojourn at the Roman
Court, that he undertook his masterpiece, the
Summa Theologiae.

In the brief Introduction, St. Thomas tells us his
intention in writing the book. During his long
career, he had covered the entire cycle of doctrinal
questions many times. He decided to assemble and
order them in a vast and ingenious synthesis. By
putting each one in its place, the various questions
are condensed, shed light on one another, and
attain their mutual perfection.

It is rather surprising to find the same well-
developed arguments in the *Commentary on the
Sentences* which were treated again more succinctly
in the *Summa.* Thomas taught, dictated, and argued
every question as many as ten or twenty times.
Nothing is more instructive nor more important
than following the genesis and development of
Thomas' thought in the chronological order of his
works. We would be mistaken, then, to attribute
an opinion to St. Thomas on causality, analogy, the
sacraments, or the agent intellect which he put
forth in the *Commentary on the Sentences,* but
corrected and amended in his later works. The
Summa is a synthesis, a coördination of the truths
which previously had been rather scattered and
unorganized.

Seen in its totality, the *Summa* is a synthesis of
the philosophy and theology accumulated in two

very different and sometimes divergent civiliza-
tions. The greatest title of glory attributed by the
history of human thought to Thomas Aquinas will
be that he reconciled Greek philosophical humanism
with Judaeo-Christian revelation. As we have indicated above, the Roman popes assumed part of the
responsibility for this work, which they wisely and
vigilantly protected.

St. Thomas did not compose this masterpiece in
the serenity of his cell at Rome. Although the plan
was conceived and even begun at the convent of
Santa Sabina, the greatest part of it was completed
at Paris in the years from 1269 to 1272. Since we
have chosen a particularly historical point of view
in this study, we ought to mention the philosophical
and religious agitation which surrounded Thomas
at Paris.

Brother Thomas was teaching at Viterbo in the
Roman Court, which had been convened in that
city by the Pope, when suddenly he was sent back
to the convent of Saint-Jacques in Paris. Although
no reason is advanced in the chronicles for this
transfer, their silence is telling. In reading the early
history of the Preachers, when a Master General,
a prelate, or an eminent doctor belonging to the
Order left Rome or the Pontifical Court without
any reason being recorded in the chronicles, we
can be certain that the Curia exerted its influence
in the affair. Thomas was then the most excellent

theologian in the Curia. If his new assignment was not decided by the cardinals, they at least must have approved it.

The work of reconciliation between Aristotelianism and Christian revelation commanded by the popes was not being carried out. The secular masters and the Franciscan school vehemently opposed any introduction of Peripateticism into the University of Paris. On the other hand, the young students of the faculty of arts, under the direction of intelligent but bold and foolhardy masters, accepted Aristotle wholly and, what is worse, understood him as interpreted by Averroes. As we have said, Pope Alexander IV asked Albert the Great to write a tract against Averroism. In 1263, when Thomas undertook his critical studies of the texts of Aristotle, Pope Urban IV renewed the prohibition on teaching the uncorrected texts of Aristotle. Nevertheless, the Faculty of Arts used these books, which had never been corrected in the twenty years since Rome had promised it. Cries of Averroism were heard everywhere. At this time, somewhere between the years 1260 and 1270, an intelligent and likeable young man appeared, who was to come to a very sad end.[8]

---

[8]Siger of Brabant has left behind him some philosophical works, which, even though they are totally Averroistic, are of prime value. He calls Albert the Great and St. Thomas *praecipuii viri in philosophia.* On the particular point of the

Judging from his works, Siger of Brabant, the young Master of Arts from Flanders, appeared as the only one capable of seconding St. Thomas Aquinas. With his friend Boethius of Dacia, he was the leader of the younger students who composed the Faculty of Arts, some of whom had accepted the ultra-Aristotelian or Averroist position.

This studious youth was risking great danger. He was tempted to give up belief in the immortality of the individual soul, free will, and the merit of good actions. It was equally impossible to repress this mounting tide of Averroism either by reinforcing the ancient strongholds of prohibitions or by maintaining the ultra-traditionalist position of the Platonic-Augustinians.

On the other hand, the theological method of the Dominicans, begun by Albert the Great and followed by St. Thomas, lacked proponents at Paris; and because of its Aristotelian characteristics it ran the risk of being confused with the Averroist position. At the same time, the struggles were re-

possible intellect being deprived of all species and able to receive them all, he admits that he hesitated for a long time and finally had recourse to faith. In concluding, he declares that he did not solve the question whether science belongs to the first species of quality, in order that the reader may be impelled to study, to read, to be alert regarding this difficulty, for he adds: "Without letters life is dead, and the tomb of a man is vile." The quotation is no less beautiful for being borrowed from Seneca. See Mandonnet, *Siger de Brabant*, II, p. 171.

newed between the secular masters, the friends of William of Saint-Amour, and the Preachers. This is the reason why Thomas returned so suddenly from the Roman Court in Italy. And the secular masters were only too happy to get an opportunity for revenge. The Bishop of Paris, Stephen Tempier, and the Franciscans supported the seculars in the battle against Peripateticism. They added to the condemnation of Aristotle and Averroism at least two of Thomas' own theses: the unity of substantial forms and the possible creation of the world *ab aeterno*.

When Thomas arrived at Paris, he found two opposing groups of adversaries. On the left were the ultra-Aristotelians or Averroists, and on the right were the ultra-traditionalists, the Platonic-Augustinians. His battle with each would be tricky and violent.

In their naïve simplicity, thirteenth-century chroniclers record the most distressing events with an equanimity that inevitably puts us off our guard and forces us constantly to refer to other sources. The secretary of the King of Sicily, Bartholomew of Capua, relates the following in the process of canonization:

In theological disputes, when men usually go to extremes, Thomas always remained quiet and humble. One day he disputed in the presence of John Peckham, later the Archbishop of Canterbury. Although Peckham exasperated Thomas with injurious and proud words (*verbi ampullosis et tumidis*), Thomas kept speaking softly and answering with humility.[9]

This sounds more like a description of a class exercise or "circle" than a real debate.

We possess another account of the dispute, one written by John Peckham himself. At the time, Thomas was Regent at the convent of Saint-Jacques and John Peckham was Regent of the Franciscans. The debate was attended by the Bishop of Paris and a great number of students. These solemn public discussions were held frequently to consider the most pressing difficulties of the day. The masters present were permitted to make any objection they wished on any subject whatever. For this reason, the contraversies or disputes were called *quodlibets*. It is likely that the discussion in question took place around Easter of 1270. At least, it is absolutely certain that the session was very solemn and very important. The whole tenor of the account in the writings of Peckham and even the evidence of the ignorant witnesses seem to indicate that this was one of the most memorable theological disputes of the thirteenth century.

John Peckham's report should be examined very closely:

When Brother Thomas was contradicted with the utmost force (*argueretur argute*) by the Bishop of

[9]Boll., *Acta Sanctorum* (VII Mars), I, p. 710.

Paris, by the masters in Theology, and by his own Brothers, we alone came to his aid, defending him as much as we could without wounding the truth. So that in the end, Brother Thomas, like the humble doctor he was, submitted himself and all his positions to the judgment (*moderamini*) of the masters of Paris for a correction which could have been imminent.[10]

As head of the Franciscan school, it is unlikely that John Peckham came to the aid of Brother Thomas Aquinas, so that he could be called his protector. We know from other sources that his school was passionately opposed to the Dominican approach in theology. The Preachers and Friars Minor were brother enemies.[11]

As we shall see later, when John Peckham was made Archbishop of Canterbury, he became the most rigorous and most opinionated censor of Thomas' work. And the most notable point of opposition was the very subject debated that day. The patronizing attitude which Peckham took was contradicted by the testimony of Bartholomew of Capua, who noted that the Franciscan Master had done all he could to exasperate Thomas by calling his doctrine heretical, scandalous, absurd, and Averroistic.

[10]Cited by Mandonnet, *op. cit.*, p. 99.

[11]It would be unpleasant to dwell on the doctrinal antagonism between the Preachers and Friars Minor. John Peckham himself stated that the doctrinal theses of the two Orders were fundamentally and generally opposed: "Cum doctrina duorum ordinum in omnibus dubitalibus sibi pene penitus hodie adversetur."

It is still less believable, if even possible, that Thomas Aquinas, Regent of the Friars Preachers, holding the Chair of Theology at the convent of Saint-Jacques, envied by the heads of the University who wanted to suppress him, would have submitted his theses to the correction of the secular masters. Such a deed would have indicated that Thomas, theologian of the Pope and the Roman Curia, had completely lost his restraint. The submission of a Dominican master to the "regime" of the University would at the very least have been extremely imprudent.

The testimony of the witnesses at the process of canonization was right. John Peckham attacked the most vulnerable theses of Thomas' teaching, because they were the most controversial, and were, moreover, the points held in common by both Thomas and Averroes. Peckham was supported by the Bishop of Paris, who entered the arena and attacked Thomas, by all the masters of the University, and also—alas!—very likely by a certain number of his own Dominican brethren. And if Peckham pushed his offensive as far as he could, it was because he knew that, with the right help, a condemnation, a "correction could be imminent." The Bishop of Paris prepared the condemnation of Averroism; and it would be issued a few months later. Those at the University and the Franciscans would have been happy to add to the condemned theses the one concerning the unity of substantial forms, which was shared by both Thomas and Siger de Brabant. This thesis would have been condemned by Bishop Stephen Tempier, in order to discredit Thomistic doctrine and the Aristotelian method. It would have been the revenge of the secular masters and a victory for the Friars Minor over the Preachers.

But the Regent of Saint-Jacques, Thomas Aquinas, knew perfectly well what he was doing.[12] Although most of the theologians of the old school were against him, Thomas had friends and collaborators. Besides, he did not count on anyone's help. Nor was he shaken from his customary serenity for an instant. It is easy to picture him in his chair, wearing his black cape, with his doctoral cap turned down as far as his ears, abstracted from all this confusion and insult, his forehead a little wrinkled, the only one trying to understand the matter clearly. No, he needed no one to second him, and no one was capable of it. He took all the attacks head-on. He could answer all the objections of

[12]There is evidence that St. Thomas and the Dominicans knew of the imminent condemnation of the Averroistic propositions and the possible condemnation of Thomas' theses. Giles of Lessines, a Dominican, sent a letter to Albert the Great, begging him to give his judgment on the thirteen propositions which were going to be condemned, plus two others taught by Thomas which were likely to be included: the unity of substantial forms and the simplicity of spiritual substances. If these last propositions, especially the unity of substantial forms, were not condemned, it was only because Thomas defended them with as much wisdom and intelligence as energy.

John Peckham and the secular masters. And if, as he would later do at the moment of his death, he submitted "all his positions" to a master, it was not to the masters of the University who were the downfall of his Order, but to the Master of the Roman Church. As humble as the appeal was, it must have frightened the masters and the Bishop of Paris. They knew how vigilant and energetic the Pope and cardinals could prove themselves.

In the following month of December, 1270, the Bishop of Paris and the masters of the University condemned the Averroistic theses upheld by Siger of Brabant and Boethius of Dacia. The thesis on the unity of substantial forms, attacked by John Peckham and the secular masters, was not included. Thomas Aquinas had removed it. For two years, he opposed both the Averroist and the conservative proponents of Augustinianism. In two works written during this time, *De aeternitate mundi contra murmurantes* and *De unitate intellectus,* we see the athlete of Faith in full combat with two opposing sides, cutting and thrusting, adding an ironic taunt after every established thesis. After he showed that creation in time cannot be proved absolutely by reason, Thomas addressed these words to the dyed-in-the-wool conservatives, the *murmurantes*: "Ergo illi qui tam subtiliter eam percipiunt, soli sunt homines, et cum eis oritur sapientia." In reply to Siger of Brabant, the young and imprudent Master of

Arts, who inculcated his secret and esoteric theories in the minds of the young, Thomas proved that Averroes was not the "Commentator" but the corruptor (*depravator*) of Aristotle:

> Such are the facts which we have written to destroy the error (Averroism), based not only on the teaching of faith, but on arguments and quotations from the philosophers themselves. If, for the false glory of science, someone attempts to write against the truths which we have established, may he not teach it in corners before children incapable of making a sound judgment on such difficult questions, but let him write a tract publicly, if he dares. He will be answered not only by me, the least of all, but by others who have cultivated truth and who know how to refute his error and counsel his ignorance.[13]

It is important to note that Thomas does not limit himself to refuting the Averroistic errors with arguments from faith, but cites the authority of the philosophers themselves, especially Aristotle. At that time he had an excellent translation of the philosopher's works, and took a purely critical and rational position in his refutation of Averroes and Siger of Brabant. His fine distinction between the domain of faith and reason was new. It contradicted the customs of the old school which joined and confused the methods of the two Orders. On the other hand,

[13]St. Thomas Aquinas, "De unitate intellectus contra Averroistas," n. 268, *Opuscula Philosophica* (Rome: Marietti, 1954), p. 90.

Siger of Brabant and the Averroists separated reason
from faith so as to admit flagrant contradictions
between them (the principle of double truth). They
claimed to be able to teach theses of Aristotelian
philosophy contrary to Christianity, such as fatalism,
the eternity of the world, the mortality of individual
souls, and to uphold at the same time Christian
beliefs in free will, creation in time, and the
immortality of the soul. But they could not escape
the logical conclusions of such inconsistency. The
Averroists soon began to consider Christian revelation as a popular and symbolic creation. Thomas'
position comes to light in contrast to the teachings
of his adversaries. Unlike the Augustinians, he distinguishes reason from faith; but he does not make them
contraries. Against the Averroists, he holds that reason cannot prove anything contrary to faith, thus
attributing a relative autonomy to science. He does
not confuse or separate faith and reason; he distinguishes them.

From this open, central, and integral position,
which he had made his own, St. Thomas Aquinas
repelled all the attacks of his adversaries. His genius
and virtue commanded respect. Two years before
his death, in 1272, Thomas was recalled to Rome.
His departure from Paris and especially his death
renewed the strength of the secular masters. They
worked harder than ever to have several of the
Thomistic doctrines condemned as suspect of Aver-

roism. The Dominicans needed the influence of a famous man. When he heard of the premature death of his illustrious disciple, Albert the Great came from Cologne to Paris for the precise purpose of defending his violently incriminated doctrine. The journey, attested to by a witness at the process of canonization, cannot be dated with certainty.

Albert the Great could spend only a short time at Paris. After his departure, the opposition rallied its forces. As we said above, the new Thomistic school was attacked not only by the secular masters of the faculty of theology, the Bishop of Paris, and the Franciscans, but even by some Dominicans, especially those belonging to the Order's first generation. One of them, the most famous, Robert Kildwardby, a student and later Master of Arts at the University of Paris, received into the Order by Blessed Jordan of Saxony, Provincial for more than ten years in England, an austere and pious Religious, finally promoted by Gregory X, in 1272, to the Archiepiscopal See at Canterbury, the Primate of England was an intransigent enemy of Thomistic doctrine. Around the end of the year 1270, to the beginning of 1271, when the doctrinal struggles were at their height, when Kildwardby was Provincial of England, he was passing through Paris on his way to the General Chapter at Montpellier. The Acts of the chapter call him the great master of theology, *magnus magister in theologia.* Robert Kildwardby was then the most influential member of the Platonic-Augustinian tradition. He had divided and annotated a great part of Augustine's works. The coming of the Aristotelian method was a defeat for him. It is understandable that he would view Thomistic doctrine with incredible severity.

When they met at the University of Paris, Robert Kildwardby and Stephen Tempier discovered that they both held similar views on questions of doctrine. At that time, Pope John XXI ordered an investigation of the whole question of Averroism, which was again threatening the souls of the young students. The time was ripe. Both bishops prepared a condemnation of the Averroistic theses, implicating Thomistic doctrine along with them. In order that there be no mistake about their intentions, the decree was promulgated at Paris by Stephen Tempier, on the seventh of March, 1277, three years to the day after Thomas' death. Ten years later, Robert Kildwardby, as Bishop of Canterbury and Primate of England, would condemn Averroism and implicate the Thomistic doctrines, especially that of the unity of substantial forms. Both prelates claimed to have previously acquired the agreement of the masters of theology at the Universities of Paris and Oxford; this was certainly true of Oxford.

At Paris, Thomas Aquinas had partisans among the masters of the Dominican house and in the Faculty of Arts. The preparatory Faculty, which was composed of the youngest students, was quite large. St. Thomas had the youth on his side. Shortly after his death, on May 2, 1274, the Faculty of Arts requested that the Master General of the Dominicans surrender the body and writings of the Saint to them. In this request, an enthusiastic eulogy praised the doctor with the well-deserved title of "morning light or rather the greatest light of full day, shining on the Church with all its brightness."[14] In the severe view of the theologians of the University of Paris, nothing was more likely to provoke condemnation than the enthusiasm of these young students, some of whom had lost their faith following Siger of Brabant.

But Thomas had more powerful and influential admirers than the University students. We have already spoken of the esteem in which he was held at the Roman Court, where he had taught for ten years. His works, his methods, and his teaching had been encouraged and approved by cardinals and popes. Thomas Aquinas was Italian. The Curia was proud of his nobility, his knowledge, and his virtue. He was a *persona grata*. The cardinals were gathered at Anagni to elect a successor to John XXI, when they learned that Stephen Tempier was planning an explicit condemnation of Thomas' method and teaching. They were already displeased with the preceding censures and commanded the Bishop of

[14]H. Denifle, *Chartularium Universitatis Parisiensis,* n. 447, I, p. 504.

Paris to forego any immediate action. Tempier was probably trying to profit from the six-month vacancy of the Holy See, but the Roman Curia proved much more vigilant and energetic than he had presumed.

The cardinals appointed a Dominican prelate, Peter Conflans, Archbishop of Corinth and resident of the Roman Court, to intervene with the Primate of England. He wrote a rather strong letter to Robert Kildwardby, reproaching him for the condemnation of Thomas Aquinas. Robert Kildwardby was as stubborn as he was authoritarian. Earlier, as Provincial of England, he was removed from office by the Chapter of Barcelona and exiled to Germany, because he had refused to accept Brothers from foreign countries assigned by the Order to the convent at the University of Oxford. He was exiled, but re-elected by all his Religious. A powerful person, Kildwardby was closed to doctrinal innovation. His answer to the Archbishop of Corinth was worded strongly. He began with a small lesson in precision by pointing out that the condemnation did not include a decree of heresy, but only prohibition. After this, he justified the interdict by affirming that he "condemned (the works) with the consent of all the masters, both regents and non-regents, of the University of Oxford." The prohibited theses were, "either manifestly false, or contrary to true philosophy, or approach intolerable errors, or evidently evil, because they are contrary to the Catholic faith (*apertissime iniqui, quia fidei catholicae repugnantes*)."[15]

We are not so surprised by this description of Thomas' teaching when we recall that the masters gained an indulgence for not teaching his doctrine. In the words of Occam, the Thomistic thesis on the unity of substantial forms had begun an almost infinite scandal in Oxford and the schools of England: "scandalum prope infinitum."[16]

In March, 1278, Robert Kildwardby was elevated to the dignity of cardinal and called to Italy. This reminds us of the famous principle of the Roman Curia: *Promovetur ut amoveatur*. He was replaced in the see of Canterbury by a Friar Minor, John Peckham. The former Regent of the Franciscan school of Paris, it was Peckham who claimed to have come to the aid of Thomas Aquinas at a moment when he needed a helping hand. In 1282, when he enlarged the condemnation of Thomism published by Robert Kildwardby, Peckham was only

[15]Cited in Mandonnet, *op. cit.*, p. 235.

[16]This is the literal text of Occam's testimony: "I have often heard many Englishmen and Britons explaining Thomas' opinion on the unity of form, when the conclusions which flow from it were explained, the scandal in England is almost infinte" (Mandonnet, *ibid.*, p. 237). At that time, when theology and philosophy were not sufficiently distinguished, they could not understand how St. Thomas' thesis of the unity of forms could be reconciled with the real corporality of the body of our Lord in the tomb. Albert the Great had already answered that it was necessary to separate the two theses and not to judge mysteries by natural reason.

following the impetus begun by his Order. In 1282, a General Chapter of the Friars Minor had forbidden the reading of the *Summa* in Franciscan schools. Despite the prohibitions, Thomism grew. Richard Clapwel, a Dominican, even taught it at Oxford. John Peckham summoned him to his archiepiscopal tribunal, but the Preacher invoked the exemptions of his Order.

They continued to argue, attack, and condemn. It would take fifty years of battle for the Thomistic doctrine to be recognized canonically. The event which put an end to all the argument was the canonization of Thomas Aquinas on July 18, 1323. Two years later the prohibitions levied against the Aristotelian and Thomistic method were lifted by the Bishop of Paris. Again it was the Pope and the Roman Curia, who, by canonizing Thomas, took the first step toward the official recognition of Thomism as the doctrine of the Catholic Church.

These historic considerations are necessary for a more accurate understanding of the principal meaning of the canonization of St. Thomas. They prepare the ground for a truer knowledge of his apologetic and doctrinal work, which manifests a double character and intention. St. Thomas fought for religious and monastic life to his very last days, one might say to his death, since he died on his journey to the Council of Lyons where the question of religious life was being discussed. This essential point of his apologetic activity is usually overlooked. In 1270, while at Paris, against the secular masters of the University, especially Gerard d'Abbeville and Nicholas of Lisieux, he wrote *De perfectione vitae spiritualis contra pestiferam doctrinam retrahentium homines a religionis ingressu.* It seems that religious and monastic life will always have its enemies.

The Christian and non-Christian world has rightly given most of its attention to the book which combines St. Thomas' philosophical, theological, and scriptural activity, his *Summa Theologiae.* We cannot stress too strongly the fact that this masterpiece was not composed in the passivity of solitary contemplation, but at the height of a prodigiously active existence. The famous story, which tells of Thomas in the palace of King Louis IX, rapping his fist on the table, and crying out, "There's the final argument against the Manichaeans," conceals a deeper meaning than is ordinarily recognized. St. Thomas was truly an athlete of the faith, (*pugil fidei*—πύξ fist). He continued apologetically the campaign begun by his Father Dominic, constantly fighting his enemies in every camp. In battle, he was humble, magnanimous, and strong. According to William of Tocco, he was also "the most patient of men (*patientissime*)." Pierre Dubois calls him "the most prudent of men (*prudentissime*)."

In the following chapter, we propose to investigate how virtue in St. Thomas Aquinas contributed to the understanding of integral truth. From his intellectual and doctrinal career, there remains this great lesson. New doctrines are combated victoriously, not by insisting on keeping out-of-date opinions unchanged, but by striving to assimilate the qualities of method and the valuable truth which these new doctrines bring with them. For, each century carries with it new elements which it must assimilate, at least in part. The purpose of the *Summa* was to augment traditional doctrine by adapting new methods and new findings.

Three: SPIRITUAL LIFE

There seems to be a significant omission in the canonization process of St. Thomas Aquinas. During the Middle Ages, and especially toward the end of the thirteenth century, the lives of saints and blesseds consisted, for the most part, in an endless round of flagellations, macerations, and bloody penances. Yet we find nothing of the kind in the first biographies and testimonies of the life of St. Thomas. We might question whether this omission arises from ignorance or an oversight. Reading the lives of Thomas Aquinas by William of Tocco, Tolomeo of Lucca, and Bernard of Guy, and reviewing the testimonies of the witnesses at the process of canonization, we cannot find a single chapter or even an important paragraph concerning violent mortifications. Nevertheless we are convinced that St. Thomas was interiorly one of the most mortified of ascetics. Our task will be to establish the veracity of this assertion.

It is no less a fact that Thomas' mortification was different from that practiced by other Dominican saints of his time. There were no hair shirts, iron chains, disciplines or bloody macerations like the ones we read of in the lives of the first Friars Preachers. In fact, there are not even any legends of bodily penances, whose exaggerations and creations are themselves often quite revealing. They indicate the direction and development of a saint's character and temperament. Legends are magnanimous. They bestow riches on those who are not rich. Thomas' mother is a good example. History tells us that she was entrenched in feudal prejudice. William of Tocco, who would not have known this, ingeniously tries to make us believe that the Countess had Thomas arrested at Acquapendente because of a simple misunderstanding with the Dominicans of Naples. Tocco tells us that the Countess Theodora "was very self-mortifying, so much so that she not only had calluses on her knees [that was common enough] but also on her hands, because of her frequent prostrations." We know that pious persons of the Middle Ages frequently multiplied inclinations and prostrations. According to William of Tocco, St. Thomas' sister, the Countess of San Severino, "was so rigorous that she devoted a great part of the night to inflicting herself with most painful penances, using an iron chain (*catena ferrea*)."[1]

William of Tocco, who mentions the mortifica-

[1] Boll., *Acta Sanctorum* (VII Mars), I, p. 670.

tions of Thomas' mother and sister, fails to mention any like penances in the life of the Saint himself. His disciples, the witnesses at the canonization, when asked under oath to vouch for penances concerning Brother Thomas, were constrained to remain silent. If there are no legends reporting calluses on his hands or primitive disciplines with iron chains, it is only because his disciples and confidants testified that such penances were not used by St. Thomas. It would be extreme to say that Thomas did not take the discipline according to the common rule. But there are none of the violent and bloody practices so common among the Dominicans of the thirteenth century. Since we have advanced the notion that Thomas' asceticism was as profound and real as that of the saints who preceded him, it follows that this asceticism was both new and at the same time traditional. Should it be surprising that St. Thomas, who represents a new monastic discipline and introduced a new theological method, would spontaneously renovate traditional asceticism.

An evolution of asceticism has taken place. Here more than elsewhere, we must emphasize the role of the individual. For nothing is more one's own, more original or more dependent on temperament, than asceticism. In all times, in all places, and under all conditions we find ascetics who practice frightening penances. Statistics here are meaningless. But, if we devote less attention to the individual, and concentrate on the entire history of monastic life, it is evident that asceticism changes in proportion to the degree that monastic life itself has progressed. The asceticism of the Benedictine colonizer or explorer clearing virgin forests could not have been the same as that of Theobald. The asceticism of the Preachers was not that of the Benedictines, the Cistercians, or the Carthusians. Numerous individual exceptions do not destroy the general principle. The Order of Preachers was the first of the truly modern Orders. Its founder, St. Dominic, introduced the principle of dispensation into the Constitutions. Dispensations from Divine Office, from fasts, and from rising at night were necessitated by the demands of study, and were given as an aid to study. By the very fact that a monastic Order retained some of its most gifted students for higher university learning, it was inevitable that asceticism among those Religious would undergo modification. Hence for Thomas, who was and still is the model philosopher-theologian-monk, asceticism became less violent, less momentary, less bloody, less something that was just skin-deep. On the contrary, it was more profound and interior. It controlled not only his heart, but also his head. His asceticism was more intellectual. We shall attempt to determine the principal characteristics of this intellectual asceticism, found in a pre-eminent degree in St. Thomas. But first of all, we must have as clear a definition of asceticism as possible.

Asceticism is in great part physical. But certain organs of the human body, because of their immediate participation in the acts of the intellect, like the eyes and brain centers, are more intellectual, more interior and spiritual than the organs of external sensation and nutrition. The first anchorites, the Fathers of the Desert, tended to passive and intuitive affective contemplation, without distinction and composition of thoughts, similar in many ways to Neo-Platonic contemplation.[2]

The Fathers of the Desert lived in the hot climate of the Nile Valley, and supported themselves by manual labor. They were especially devoted to mortification by hunger and thirst, controlling their instinctive needs to speak and travel from place to place, needs which are deeply-rooted in human nature. We do not read of these anchorites practicing bloody flagellations like those of Henry Suso.[3]

They underwent prolonged fasts, vigils, physical immobility, and silence. Apostles, men of action like St. Paul, have the greatest need of violent and rapid penances, of rhythmic prayer with bodily move-

[2]The Desert Fathers were, from the beginning, in constant contact with Alexandria. Plotinus (d. 270) was the founder of the Neo-Platonic school of Alexandria. Porphyry was his disciple. In their teaching, ecstasy, conditioned by a certain asceticism, took the place of the Cross. The influence of Neo-Platonism and Stoicism on the Desert Fathers is incontestable. St. Nilus adapted the *Manual of Epictetus* to monastic life.

[3]See Renée Zeller, *Le B. Henri Suso.*

ments. The reason is obvious: their apostolic ministry hinders extraordinary fasts and prolonged periods of silence. They must mortify their bodies by flagellations, hair shirts, and iron disciplines.

We can see from these examples that asceticism generally consists in the practice of exercises by which the faithful or Religious restrains and subjects his brute or lower functions, in order to develop the higher spiritual faculties. Asceticism, which etymologically means exercise, reduces, suppresses, and mortifies life, at the same time that it animates it. In Christianity, asceticism is inseparable from mysticism. It tempers and redirects sense life to increase contemplative and interior life. Because the term mysticism has been reserved to the science and practice of prayer and contemplation, asceticism is especially applied as a synonym for physical mortification.

The asceticism of St. Thomas, like that of other monks devoted to higher studies, resembles the asceticism of the Desert Fathers. William of Tocco tells us that each day Thomas read a few pages of the *Conferences of Cassian with the Fathers of the Desert*. This was his manual of the ascetic life. This was the book he used to renew his fervor and dispose himself for divine speculation. But if Thomas went to the cells of the Desert Fathers to consult with Serapion, the Abbot Moses, Paphnutius, and Serenus on some mystical or ascetic subject, he did so doubtlessly to follow their teachings and to imitate their examples.[4]

The most exterior ascetic practice mentioned in the biography of St. Thomas is fasting. Reginald of Piperno, who was the most intimate confidant of the Saint, reports that the Master encountered a passage in Isaiah which he could not understand, so he mortified himself with fasts (*multis diebus afflixit se . . . jejuniis*), praying that God would reveal the hidden meaning of the Scripture. We have here an evident example of ascetic practice which is inseparable from mystical belief. Fasting was not only used as a purely physical means to favor thought, but as an act of penance agreeable to God, as a prayer of petition. Doubtlessly, Thomas used this same ascetic and mystical practice to obtain the light of the Holy Spirit in other difficulties. A Christian philosopher who is not a mystic, but solely an intellectual, will not feel moved to practice imprecatory fasts for any extended time.

Fast almost always presupposes abstinence. We read that Thomas was so temperate that he paid no

[4]See John Cassian, *Conferences with the Desert Fathers*. Since this book was one of Thomas' manuals, it must be studied to understand the ascetic character of his spiritual life. We search there in vain for references to violent and bloody penances similar to those described by Gérard de Fachet in his *Lives of the Brethren*. What we do find in Cassian is the necessity of solitude, flight from the world, silence, fast, constant contemplation, and reserve.

attention to the excellence of food (*de delicantia et singularitate ciborum*), and that he was content with the ordinary fare of the convent. This insistence that Thomas, like most of the other Religious, was satisfied by the dishes served in the refectory is surprising when we realize that the masters of theology, especially those who were regents in a studium or a university, had the right to special dispensations and favors. For the Preachers, adherence to the daily menu included the important ascetic practice of perpetual abstinence from all meat. Even on Easter, whether he was at Paris, Cologne, or Naples, Thomas ate only vegetables, fish, or eggs. A few incidents in his life show us how extensive was his observance of this Dominican rule. Thomas of Cantimpré tells us that, when the Saint was a novice imprisoned in the dungeon of his family's castle, he refused to change his diet. He put up with extreme poverty and starvation rather than quit his fasting. His jailors could not even bully him into eating the meat they set before him. There is another interesting example of his abstinence taken from the end of his religious life. A few weeks before his death, Thomas completely lost his appetite. The doctor tried to get him to take some food. Finally, the Saint admitted that he would enjoy some fresh herring like the ones eaten in France and England. The doctors and the brothers accompanying him were astounded. These herrings were not sold in this region of Italy, so it would be impossible to fulfill the Saint's wish. A peddler happened to be passing the house at this time, and by a miracle he had some of these herrings in his basket. They were prepared, dressed, fried, and even seasoned (*elixatas in brodio et etiam assatas*). This simple and naïve story, which seems authentic enough, indicates to us very clearly that Thomas Aquinas still thought only of fasting, especially since it was still Lent. These fish were undoubtedly the best food he tasted in his life.

With such confidence in fasting, Thomas must have observed all the fasts and abstinences of the Church and the Order. Except when sick or dispensed, he fasted for almost seven months of the year, a diet which seems incredible to men today. Yet it is a fact that our ancestors were less liberal than we in dispensing from the fast, and besides, habit facilitates this kind of asceticism more than is commonly believed. Then, too, we must take into account the diversity of temperaments. Orientals and Neopolitans fast and abstain more easily than the French, Germans, and Anglo-Saxons. According to William of Tocco, St. Thomas ate only once a day (*manducabet semel in die.*) This is the literal practice of fasting.[5]

---

[5]We said before that fasting was one of the principal penances used by the anchorites and cenobites of the early Church. Cassian recommended it strongly. A pound of bread was enough for an ascetic to carry with him on a journey. Solitaries could be so absorbed in contemplation that they

Besides fast and abstinence, there are other affective privations which the ascetic applies not only to vegetable life, that is, to the functions of nutrition, but also to animal functions. Locomotion is the first of these functions, because mobility is what primarily distinguishes animal from vegetable life. The need for motion is deeply-rooted in man's lower nature. It is as natural for him to move as it is for him to breathe. The anchorites violently controlled this need, because it is most opposed to the interior life. The Benedictines make a vow of stability, a vow to remain in their abbey until death. In the thirteenth century, the active Preachers found it necessary to give up the vow of stability. William of Saint-Amour criticized the unnecessary journeys of the new Preachers, and repeated the words of St. Augustine: "Nusquam missos, nusquam stantes, nusquam sedentes" ("Never sent, never standing, never sitting"). Earlier religious called this nervousness, common both to children and to men of small minds, "inquietude." The anchorites thought that the remedy for this veritable mania or sickness was seclusion, voluntary imprisonment. There were stylites who lived for years atop pillars.

would forget to eat. We can read of the unqualified extension which Thomas has given to the practice of fasting in the *Summa Theologiae*, II-II, q. 147. Fasting is twofold: spiritual and corporeal. There is the fasting of sadness and joy. It is used for three reasons, one of which is to elevate the spirit. Christ fasted to teach us how excellent a thing it is, etc.

Another ascetic privation which arose from their seclusion was silence, the mortification of the tongue, of man's need to speak and communicate. In the desert, the loneliness of the solitary was obviously a protection against the temptation to useless talking. But the anchorites were to become cenobites, monks gathered in a monastery or convent, the active hive. What a temptation there was to speak of their projects, of all they had done, seen, and learned! We constantly read of superiors and general chapters renewing the precept of silence: keep to your cell, keep the silence, the two primitive and primordial conditions of the ascetic life, certainly more essential than the fast and abstinence. From his very origins, the ascetic was a man who separated himself from society, closed himself off in a cell and kept the silence.

St. Thomas was a model of these two essential points of monastic asceticism. We have often mentioned how his quietude has become legendary. He was the Dumb Ox of Sicily. In the Religious Orders of the thirteenth century, daily recreation was not common as it is in our day. We learn from his biographers that Thomas usually was absent from recreation. He would take his recreation alone, walking slowly under the cloister, taking long strides, his head uncovered and raised toward the sky. This was his most frequent form of recreation: "uno de potissimis recreationibus corporis." He never left the convent except for important reasons. At the process of canonization, his disciples testified that they saw him leave the convent only two or three times: once at Naples, in the evening after Vespers, another time at Capua, to recommend his nephew at the court of the King. At Paris, he avoided all but the most indispensable communications. He excused himself when invited to visit King Louis, because he was intensely engrossed in his teaching and preparation of the *Summa*. When he finally did accept the King's invitation, it was only because the sovereign demanded the intervention of the prior. Thomas submitted humbly, but this was a unique (*semel*) exception. We have said that he did not like the common recreation. But, since he was extremely goodnatured, we can appreciate why his disciples would enjoy his company on their walks to the orchard (*viridario*). He would do violence to himself and accompanied them only if they promised to keep the conversation centered on an instructive or edifying subject (*aliquid historiale aut morale*).[6] Otherwise he would excuse himself and slip away to return to his cell or the chapel.

Besides the religious and mystical reasons which explain and necessitate this silence and seclusion for a monk, we find another important one, peculiar to Religious vowed to higher studies. It is formally expressed by St. Thomas himself in a letter he ad-

[6]Boll., *op. cit.*, p. 660.

dressed to a Brother John on the means of acquiring "the treasure of knowledge." Most of the advice can be reduced to the principle that it is necessary to apply oneself at all times. St. Thomas practiced the ingenious method which Newton phrased in these words: "Think about it all the time." For this reason, his exhortations inevitably return to the necessity of concentration and escape from distractions:

1) Be slow to speak.
2) Give yourself over constantly to contemplation.
3) Do not be too familiar, because familiarity distracts from the application necessary for study.
4) Shun useless comings-and-goings.

We can infer from these precepts that Thomas' seclusion and quietude were not merely a spontaneous quality of his temperament, but a conscious, methodical, and willed effort, an indispensable means for making rapid and useful progress in study. This intense and continual application, the absorption of the soul, which is necessary for a profound personal and original understanding of any subject whatever, was instituted by St. Thomas as a principle which implies the cessation of conversation, visits, and exterior communication. The Saint was uncompromising in his stand against contact with women, no matter how upright they may have been. He was extremely shocked (*quamplurimum*) that Religious pledged by their state to divine speculations, could waste a great part of their time seated in the parlor in long conversations with women. Thomas shunned all friendships of this type. We have no counsels from Thomas to Philothea or even any letters like those Jordan of Saxony wrote to his spiritual daughter, Blessed Diana. Apostles and Religious devoted to the ministry, to confession and direction, can, and even must, entertain such relationships. But a theologian or philosopher like St. Thomas, trying to acquire "the treasure of knowledge," must deprive himself of much more, especially of these preoccupying relationships.[7]

If the object of asceticism is to discipline certain parts of human nature in order to develop higher areas, then that must be a more elevated, cruel, and meritorious asceticism which restrains and suppresses certain cerebral centers to favor others. This is truly intellectual asceticism.

There is a necessary mortification of curiosity, not only of that vain curiosity which passionately seeks out minute facts and anecdotes, but even of the more laudable curiosity which is a desire to know. Taine

[7]We have not mentioned St. Thomas' deprivation of sleep. It seems that the Saint did not think of this as a penance in the proper sense of the term. There is no doubt that Thomas had little sleep. A modern historian has written that he slept only one hour a day. This obvious exaggeration has its origin in the words of one of the Saint's disciples, a Brother Leonard, who testified that Thomas "modicam horam occupabat in sumendo cibum vel in dormiendo." The expression "modicum horam" must be translated as "a little time."

asks whether or not there is a more painful sacrifice than that of the man of studies who, in attaining maturity, must renounce certain artistic, political, literary, and scientific aptitudes in order to excel in a specialty. St. Thomas might well have said that the way to become wise is to read only one book. If he did not say these words, he certainly put them into practice. He was a man of one science and, in this sense, a man of one book.

We often tend to believe that geniuses are necessarily, fatally, and without any merit of their own, pointed on their special way. But we are deceived in this. They accept their particular calling with the necessary setbacks and sacrifices. For example, who could deny that political talents of the first order lay hidden in the genius of St. Thomas Aquinas? When he treats of social questions in his books, he does so with such good judgment and breadth of vision that we can only conclude that he was quite capable of governing. We have the implicit confirmation of this in the policy of a King and Saint, Louis IX of France. Each time that an important and delicate question was raised in his court, King Louis would have it written down and brought to Thomas during the night, so that the learned theologian, by reflection and meditation on the problem, could send him the solution the next day. His biographer says: "When Thomas applied his speculative spirit to the affairs of this world, he treated them with a discernment and wisdom which appeared divine."

When St. Thomas gave his solution to the King, he had no thoughts of entering directly into political affairs. He mortified his own curiosity, shifted his thoughts from these matters, and returned to theology. It is certain that, as theologian of the Roman Curia, living in constant contact with the Pope and cardinals, he was always a stranger to its business and intrigues. Even Thomas' closest disciples could not understand his indifference to the affairs of the Curia. Reginald said to him: "You and Bonaventure will be named cardinals, and the whole Order will rejoice." But Thomas replied:"I will never be anything but a simple Preacher." He mortified every appetite of his mind and will which might distract him from his intellectual vocation. How few men have the heroic courage for such a mortification, preferring to remain mediocre in all rather than excel in a determined branch of human activity or science!

Like most geniuses, Thomas was well-rounded. He had the potential and opportunity to develop in many areas. He let them die, preferring to be the first of theologians. Or rather, he simply followed his particular calling in response to obedience. He separated himself from the world, renounced every relation, cloistered himself in a poor cell, where he indefatigably delved into the problems of theology. He shut himself up in a tomb, wanting to know nothing of the world and its politics, so that he could devote himself to philosophy and science. But precisely therein lies the asceticism of a religious devoted to philosophical and theological studies.

We must die to many things in order to live a divine life. It has been said that the philosopher who probes to get to the center of the earth discovers the reason for many things. All the answers converge like rays on one central point. And, moreover, when he looks up from the bottom of the well which he has dug, he sees the heavens and contemplates the stars. Thomas Aquinas, cloistered in his convent, detached from the business of the earth, lived in his little cold cell as in a tomb. But this was a tomb from which he could look out upon the heavens. In his speculations, the Saint uncovered divine truths and had the insight to translate them into immortal formulas. He worked for eternity in the presence of God. Physical and intellectual asceticism contributed essentially in preparing him for the mystical contemplation of divine beauty.

The proper act of the mystical life is prayer. This is why the tracts on mysticism, which begin with a discussion of asceticism, are, in the final analysis, tracts on prayer. Most of them offer us one or more methods of prayer. Did St. Thomas follow a method of prayer? Certainly the holy Doctor had his own manner and habits of praying that he scarcely altered. But if we are using the term "method" in its strict sense, we can answer without fear of error

that St. Thomas did not create a method of meditation or prayer, as did St. Ignatius and St. Francis de
Sales.

We know that St. Dominic and his first disciples
practiced, if not a method, at least a certain manner
of putting themselves in the state of prayer, of dis-
posing themselves to contemplation. Dominic, disturbed by the battles of the day, used inclinations
and genuflections to calm the tension his apostolic
passions aroused. He was sometimes heard to cry out,
and he always finished his ascetic and mystical
exercises with a bloody discipline. Then, calmed, he
offered himself to the divine embrace. St. Thomas,
on the other hand, was endowed with a less ardent
temperament, and did not spend his day in apostolic journeys. He had no need of these vocal prayers
and gestures. We can suggest two possible reasons
for this fact. First of all, he had a very emotional
sensitivity and was troubled with sadness: "Erat
enim miro modo passibilis et ideo subito lassivo corporis turbabatur." The other explanation is a characteristic of theologians, of men given exclusively to
the study of dogma. Theological speculation is an
immediate preparation for prayer and contemplation.
Thomas did not have to use a transition method to
lead his soul from an active to a contemplative and
passive life.

Speculation and prayer in Thomas' day were in-
termingled and founded on one another. Prayer pre-

pared for speculation and vice versa. Brother Reginald says that: "Each time Thomas wished to study, to hold a discussion, to teach, write, or dictate, he had recourse first of all to private prayer. Frequently he shed tears before studying divine truths. If some doubt came to his soul, he interrupted his work to renew his prayer."[8]

It would be necessary to conclude from this that Thomas' soul was completely impregnated with mystical piety. William of Tocco says in this regard that the great Doctor's intelligence and will were subordinated to one another, not as servants, but as two equally free sisters. Reginald testified that, when Thomas was troubled by very difficult problems, he left his cell and went to the chapel, praying in tears before the Blessed Sacrament. He would then return to his cell and continue to dictate or write.

It would be difficult to cite an important text concerning the Saint's prayer life without mentioning the most significant exterior characteristic of his mystical life: the gift of tears. This unexpected tenderness of devotion is truly characteristic. We need not emphasize the fact that his biographers would have passed over this gift in silence if it did not in fact exist. The most authentic documents concerning St. Thomas Aquinas relate that he was favored with a particular tenderness of devotion which ex-

[8]Boll., *op. cit.*, p. 668.

pressed itself in tears. When he prayed to God for the solution of important doctrinal questions, Thomas would shed tears until he was sobbing (*singultu*). There is a famous story of Thomas bursting into tears during the singing of the antiphon *Media vita.* It is not so well known that each morning when he celebrated Mass, tears fell in streams down his cheeks (*totus perfundebatur lacrymis*). At Naples, on Passion Sunday, while the Saint was celebrating Mass, he appeared to be in ecstasy and tears flooded his eyes (*inundans perfusio lacrymis*). Perhaps today we do not have sufficient appreciation for the gift of tears, which fills the soul with affection, humility, and love for Christ, and with mercy for neighbor. It satisfies the heart, detaches it from the earth, purifies and enlightens the intellect.[9]

Thomas' tears were almost always accompanied by ecstasy. This was a frequent state for St. Thomas. But here again it is impossible to distinguish clearly between mystical and speculative ecstasy. Because of his asceticism and application to study, Thomas was able to abstract himself from sense experience and to enter into the state of ecstasy at will. Once, when he had to be bled, being very sensitive and dreading the opening of his vein by the infirmarian of the convent, Thomas used a type of autosuggestion by ab-

[9]In his *Conferences,* Cassian comments on the gift of tears which he valued highly. See the first conference with the Abbot Isaiah.

sorbing himself completely in theological speculations. Another time, when he had to have his leg cauterized, the Saint rested for a while on the bed, and engrossed in his speculations, did not feel the burning. This was his way of anesthetizing himself. According to the teaching of Doctor Grasset, there is a division between the higher and lower psychic functions of the brain. In certain circumstances, this division was not so radical. He could remain completely abstracted from sensation, while continuing to speak and dictate as if he had put himself in an hypnotic trance. An English copyist, Even Garnith, described this state when he testified to taking dictation from Thomas while the Saint was asleep. Once Thomas was holding a candle in his hand and was unaware that it had almost burned down to his fingers. Brother Reginald had to grab it away from him. This absorption and abstraction of mind became an almost continual state with the Master. The task of contemplating the *Summa* in its entirety, with its mass of details, divisions, questions, and articles, demanded that Thomas withdraw from the world of the senses.

This semi-natural ecstasy obviously favored mystical and contemplative ecstasy which occurred most often during the Sacrifice of the Mass. Thomas had an ardent devotion to the Blessed Eucharist. Often the server or one of the Dominicans had to tug at his vestments to get him to finish the Sacrifice. He remained immobile before the Consecrated Host in an obvious state of mystical contemplation. In these ecstasies, visions and revelations were ordinary occurrences. Unquestionably the most famous of them happened when Thomas heard Christ say: "You have written well of me Thomas." The Saint received this assurance on two different occasions. When he was living at Paris, the question of the Eucharistic Species was a point of heated debate among the masters of the University. Brother Thomas was asked to write a tract on the question. When he finished his work, he went as usual to the chapel to pray before the altar of the Blessed Sacrament. Presenting his manuscript to the Divine Master, Thomas begged God to keep him from holding any erroneous opinions in this *opusculum*. Christ answered: "You have written well of the Sacrament of my Body." At Salerno, Thomas often went to pray at the altar of St. Nicholas. At this time he was writing the third part of the *Summa*, on the Passion and Resurrection of Christ. A voice which seemed to come from the Crucifix said to him: "You have written well of me Thomas, what reward do you wish?" The Saint answered: "Only you, O Lord."

We cannot relate all of his visions in detail. The chroniclers and witnesses agree that the Saint was informed in a revelation on the subject of the text of his doctoral thesis, *Rigans montes* . . ., and that he saw his successor to the chair of theology, Master Romain, in an apparition. After a long fast made because of a difficulty in the text of Isaiah, Reginald heard Thomas speaking softly. When the Master had dictated several pages in a single effort, Reginald threw himself at Thomas' feet and begged him to confide what had just happened. Thomas made him promise to keep the story secret, saying that St. Peter and St. Paul had appeared to him. We can recall, too, the vision of the angels and the cord.

Thomas' ecstasies were more frequent than is commonly known. More than a hundred times he went to the altar of the Blessed Sacrament to ask Christ whether or not some question in the *Summa* was in conformity with the truth. The *Summa Theologiae* was as much the fruit of prayer and contemplation as of study and speculation. Not once did the Saint begin work without kneeling in prayer to ask for enlightenment.

St. Thomas experienced other mystical phenomena besides the gift of tears and ecstasies. Several times, especially when Christ confirmed his teaching, he was not only in ecstasy, but he was elevated from the floor, literally assumed. One of these levitations took place in the chapel of the convent of Saint-Jacques at Paris. He was raised high off the ground. Learning of the marvel, the prior and Religious present in the convent came running. They witnessed the miracle and testified to the fact at the process of canonization.[10]

We know that phenomena of this type are far from unheard-of in the lives of the mystics. When we find well-balanced, observant, informed souls, who are very suspicious of their own opinions, who rely completely on the advice of their directors— saints like Theresa and Mother Marie du Bourg—relate the conditions, place, and time when they levitated, and when these accounts are substantiated by reliable witnesses, we are less inclined to make a categorical rejection than we could of accounts from less trustworthy sources. In the order of mystical phenomena, it is better to admit that our reason is easily confounded.

These ecstasies, levitations, and revelations represent a noteworthy quality in Thomas' character. While his asceticism was less violent, more interior, and, in a sense, more intellectual than that of most saints, his ecstasies were always specified by a genuine vision. They were ordained to the knowledge of divine truths and belonged in some way to the

[10]"Ad quod prodigium intuendum Priorem conventus et plures alios Fratres quibus revelatum erat hoc mirabile, pro testimonio vocaverunt" (Boll., *op. cit.*, p. 647). From an historical point of view, such an account has greater guarantee of authenticity than most of the events which we accept without difficulty. But we are so engulfed in a sensible and sluggish world that we are astonished by such events. We can more easily imagine the elevation of a Host than the levitation of a grown man, as if Divine Omnipotence depended on our concepts of weight and measure.

visual order. They remained intellectual rather than affective. We do not hear of phenomena in the life of the Saint which are principally or totally affective, such as transverberation, exchange of hearts, or the stigmata. This type of mystical experience includes little or nothing of the speculative. We have pointed out how delicate and abundant was the Doctor's tenderness. But wonder and awe always entered into his tears. As we know, wonder is very near to art. Some sensitive and artistic persons who contemplate the beauties of the earth, a sunset on the ocean, an aurora borealis, cannot hold back their tears. Claude le Lorrain, in ecstasy before a wide and magnificent landscape, was filled with tears. We should have no difficulty in seeing how divine mysteries could arouse such intense wonder in a mystical theologian that he would be moved to tears. Wonder, the gift of tears, contemplation, and ecstasy are the states of soul most common to St. Thomas.

We cannot treat of these favors without mentioning the *sine qua non of* Thomas' virtue: his extraordinary humility. St. Theresa wrote: "I have never received exceptional graces which did not make me profoundly humble." This law of the mystical life has no exceptions. We do not find in the life of St. Thomas the pious exaggerations of humility which are so astonishing in the lives of saints like Louis Bertrand and Catherine of Siena, who thought themselves the hated outcasts of humanity, the cause of all its evils. In his prudent way, Thomas avoided all pious exaggerations. If any saint could reconcile the just mean of natural morality with the Gifts of the Holy Spirit, it certainly was St. Thomas. He practiced in his own life the synthesis which he later established in theory between the just mean of Peripatetic ethics and the heroic virtues of Christianity. His humility was without violence or excess. It was precisely because he dealt with mysteries far above human understanding that he realized so clearly his basic powerlessness. He understood better than anyone except St. Augustine the gratuitous nature of grace and the absolute weakness of human nature corrupted by sin. Knowing that he possessed nothing of his own which he had not first received, he was not boastful of the free gifts he did receive, nor did he fail to recognize them as such. His humility was essentially true, sincere, and simple. There was nothing constrained or laborious about it.

In one of his public courses, and in front of all his students, Thomas recognized frankly and thanked God that he had never consciously yielded to the first movement of pride. If ever the least temptation to complacence came to his mind, he spontaneously and consciously rejected it. To measure the value of this humility, we must call to mind that, from the very moment of his birth, Thomas entered a life of glory. One of the most outstanding signs of this glory was that his name is mentioned along with Albert the Great and Aristotle. This sort of nominal authority was a flagrant violation of the customs of the time. It shows the incomparable prestige of the man who later was called the common doctor (*doctor communis*).[11]

We recall also that Thomas belonged to one of the highest of the noble families, that he won success after success in his studies, that at the age of thirty he was the most sought after professor in the University of Paris, the defender of his Order at the Papal Court. And yet we honor him for his constant humility. How many superior men proved unable to withstand the test of so much glory? It is hard to tell how much humility and modesty, which is basically the middle way, he brought to his search for truth. Every excess is exclusive. If Thomas had not been perfectly humble, he would never have been able to distinguish the true teachings of his adversaries from the false without excluding some part of the truth. Is not this unified and simple modesty in such a genius as much a prodigy as the extraordinary privileges

[11]This title, *doctor communis*, was clearly explained by Bartholomew of Capua, who wrote: "In scriptis ipsius communis veritas invenitur, communis claritas, communis illuminatio, communis ordo" ("In his writings we find the common truth, the common clarity, the common interpretation, and the common order"). Thomas was called the common doctor because of the accessibility of his teaching. Duns Scotus was called *doctor subtilis*, Occam, *doctor invincibilis,* and Durand of Saint-Pourcain, *doctor resolutissimus.* Is there a better name for St. Thomas than *doctor communis?*

related in the preceding pages? This was the modesty with which St. Thomas wrote the *Summa*. And if God lifted him bodily above the earth, he did so only because Thomas was so profoundly humble.

Asceticism, mysticism joined with theological speculation and meditation on the Holy Scriptures, produced more results than the *Summa* and his other philosophical and theological works. We are referring to the Office of Corpus Christi, which can be treated here only briefly.

The masterpiece of Thomas' mystical writings is the Office of the Blessed Sacrament, which Pope Urban IV commissioned him to compose for the then recently-instituted feast of Corpus Christi.[12]

It is rather difficult to imagine an Aristotelian scholastic who could compose hymns and lessons in classical and ornate Latin verse in metrical patterns. One would suppose that at least much planning and numerous drafts were required to produce such an orderly work of art. Yet this was not the case. As soon as the Saint knew what he wanted to say, he began writing, and composed one of the greatest masterpieces of its kind. How true it is that Christian geniuses are much more complex and excel in many more aptitudes than we suppose.

[12]The legend which tells of Urban IV asking both St. Thomas and St. Bonaventure to compose this Office is only a fable. St. Bonaventure did not have to destroy a work which he never produced.

The success of this Christian masterpiece was immediate, long-lasting, unique, and unprecedented. Except for the catechism prayers, there are no hymns, tropes, antiphons, or prayers better known to Catholics than those which make up the Office of Corpus Christi: the *Tantum Ergo, O Salutaris, Panis Anglicus, Lauda Sion,* etc. No poet, artist, composer, or writer would ever dare to dream of such prodigious success. This is certainly the work of a master. Perhaps we have exaggerated these considerations, but if with Bergson we propose that the most infallible sign of the excellence of a work is its success in space and time, if we agree with Taine that the greatest value should be attributed to the most profoundly and most universally beneficial masterpiece, then we can only say that the Office of Corpus Christi is one of the rarest and most valuable masterpieces of humanity.

The reader should not rely solely on my meager commentary on the hymns of Corpus Christi. Others have fulfilled this function with much more competence than I possess.[13] We wish only to mention that his formation in theological studies and the general character of his mystical life providentially predestined Thomas Aquinas to compose this Office. Raised until his fourteenth year in the famous Abbey of Monte Cassino, he was formed by the

[13]See R. Louis, "St. Thomas, Liturgist," *Revue des Jeunes* (March 10, 1920).

liturgy. He learned to love Gregorian chant and the beautiful hymns of the Office. This sensitivity for religious poetry gradually developed in his soul. Thomas' brother Reginald was one of the best poets at the court of Frederick II. Thomas' careful studies of the Messianic symbolism of the Prophets in the Old Testament, the theology of the Eucharist, and his particular devotion to the Sacrament of the Altar seemed to have prepared him from his birth to create this Office. A masterpiece of such excellence and fullness does not spring forth suddenly from the mind and heart of a man of genius without a very long and complete preparation. There is an abundance of Scripture, theology, and poetry in the Office and hymns of Corpus Christi. Only the prejudiced or unbeliever would call the rhyme and cadence of the prose dry and empty. It is religious and theological poetry tempered by the tears of contemplation.

The lessons, antiphons, hymns, and prose which form the principal parts of this Office are the interpretations of the thoughts, feelings, and even the melodies of Christian tradition. Thomas again justified his title *doctor communis.* Even before Pascal, Thomas thought that "the excellence of something does not consist in being extraordinary or bizarre, for nothing is more common than good things; it is only a question of recognizing them." Christian commonsense is nothing more than a universal religious sense, a Catholic sense. Theologian of the popes, Thomas possessed to an eminent degree this sense for truth in Catholic art. That is why the Office of Corpus Christi is the most common and well-known office in the Catholic liturgy.

The sermons of St. Thomas manifest the depth of his ascetic and mystical life. Although the orator in him was sacrificed to favor his development as a theologian and teacher, Thomas preached quite frequently. In fact, he enjoyed great renown as a preacher. He delivered his sermons at Saint-Jacques in Paris, before the Religious, the faithful, and members of the University. In Italy he preached to the Roman Court. At Naples, he spoke each night during Lent. He evoked such emotion when speaking of the Passion that he had to stop while the people wept. "If you wish me to make you cry," said the poet, "you must first cry yourself." Never was this more true than in the case of St. Thomas. His commanding presence, the aura of learning and simplicity which surrounded him, must have fascinated and charmed his listeners. William of Tocco tells us that, because of his constant abstraction of mind, Thomas could speak no other vernacular language besides his native dialect. At Naples, he used the language of the province. The biographer adds that he put aside his theological erudition and scholastic subtleties, and produced the fruits of conversion in the hearts of the people.

The sermons which we possess do not give an adequate impression of the Saint's eloquence. At Paris and Rome, he preached and delivered formal discourses in Latin before the University and the Sacred College. His academic or literary sermons are very different from his teaching style, or even from his more familiar University sermons. In the latter, we hear Thomas speak with a certain frankness, energy, and brilliant clarity. He borrowed striking examples from the Bible and common usage in a manner reminiscent of Plato. The sermon given before the Consistory at the occasion of the institution of the feast of Corpus Christi is an example of his ornate literary style. His exclamations are lyric and flowing, without the use of distinctions and divisions. Professors and the students of St. Thomas were more familiar with his second manner of exposition, in which he used divisions and the customary Latin. An example of this type of sermon is one usually called the sermon of the *vetula*, preached against the false prophets. The reason for the title will be evident in the extract cited below. Here we recognize at once St. Thomas as doctor, apostle, apologist, and Friar Preacher.

There can be found today men studying philosophy who hold opinions contrary to the faith; and when this is brought to their attention, they answer that the Philosopher [Aristotle] says these things, and that they are merely stating his opinions, that they themselves affirm nothing. Such a man is a false prophet, a false doctor. For to raise a doubt without resolving it is the same thing as to concede it. It is said in Exodus that, if a man digs a well or opens a cistern, and does not cover it up afterwards, and if the ox of a neighbor happens to fall into the cistern, he who has opened the cistern is bound to make reparation. He who raises a doubt about these things which concern faith is like the man who opens a cistern; he who does not resolve this doubt, even though he be of sound and clear mind and not easily led into error, is like the man who does not cover up the cistern. One whose mind is not as clear may easily be led into error, and the one who has first raised the doubt is bound to make reparation, for it is through his doing that the other man has fallen into the well. Understand this: there have been many pagan philosophers who have said many things concerning the truths of the faith, and scarcely will you ever find two of them who hold the same opinion. And if any one of them has said something true, it was with an admixture of error. An old woman (*vetula*) today knows more about the truths of the faith than all the philosophers of the past put together. We read that early in his life Pythagoras was an athlete. Then he heard a master talking about the immortality of the soul, and was so moved (*allectus*) by this that he left everything for the study of philosophy. But where is the old woman (*vetula*) today who does not know that the soul is immortal? Faith is far more valuable than philosophy. Thus, if philosophy is contrary to faith, it must be rejected.[14]

It must have been a beautiful sight to see Thomas,

[14]See St. Thomas Aquinas, *Opera Omnia,* ed. Parma, XXIV, pp. 227-28. The text is that taken down at the time of the sermon by one of those present. Our translation is as literal as we can make it, preserving the repetition of certain words.

the athlete, *pugil,* grasping Aristotelian philosophy
and hurling it to the feet of faith. Students flocked
to his chair as Preacher as they did to his chair as
Master. This sermon concerned a burning issue. Full
of life and fire, it leads us back to events which
are familiar to us. Had not the secular masters,
friends of William of Saint-Amour, accused the Religious, the Preachers of Saint-Jacques, of being the
false prophets, the precursors of the Antichrist? St.
Thomas led them before his chair and boldly explained his position as was the custom in the Middle
Ages. Were not the distinction, the separation and
the union of reason and faith also the great questions
of methodology in scholastic theology? He knocked
his fist no longer on the table as he did in the presence of the King, but on the side of his chair against
those adorers of Aristotle, Averroes, and philosophy.
"A contemporary old woman knows more than all the
philosophers together." Doubtlessly the greatest doctor of thirteenth-century Peripateticism was competent enough to say this. But would he have preferred
faith to reason, revelation to speculation, and in-
spiration to reasoning if he had not been a mystic
and a saint?

Whatever has been said about him, Thomas
was not merely an intellectualistic theologian. The
process of canonization affirms this by recalling
many examples of his faith, prayer, and piety. In
this sense, Thomas' testimony that prayer is superior

to reason is authenticated by his disciples and officially recognized by the Church's sanction in the very canonization itself.

There is nothing left to complete the interior life of St. Thomas except a consideration of his death. For the death of a saint is not only precious in the sight of the Lord, but provides rich teachings for men. Before we consider the general characteristics of the Saint, we should add a few which we have so far omitted. Toward the end of his life, Thomas changed slightly. William of Tocco, who got to know Thomas quite well in the two years before he died, tells us that the Saint always stood very straight, with a slight suggestion of stiffness. The chronicler adds that this posture was symbolic of the rectitude of his spirit. He had also become very large, we might say obese. But this defect was not too apparent because of his height. Baldness had reached the crown of his head, uncovering his temples and making his head look fuller and even larger. Thomas gave the impression of strength, of one who could not be easily intimidated. One day, a Neapolitan judge, an intimate friend of the Queen of Sicily, came to visit Thomas in his cell at the convent of Naples. They walked together on the long terrace overlooking the bay and the sea. The judge saw someone who looked like a negro, dressed in black, following the Saint. The Master raised his fist to the black devil saying: "How do you dare come here to tempt me?" Frightened, the demon fled and disappeared. We gather that Thomas appeared frightening, and that it would have been dangerous to fall under his fist. As is the case with robust men, he feared nothing. And despite the legend, this includes thunder, lightning, and storms at sea.[15] Once when he was in a sailboat which was about to capsize, he alone among the crew remained unafraid.

Thomas Aquinas, then, was extremely powerful and strong. We have not put enough emphasis on his large capacity for work. It has been estimated that the last three years spent at Paris were the most difficult of his career. He wrote or dictated a great part of the *Summa* and many short *opuscula,* comprising about twenty-three hundred pages. Such prodigious writing makes us realize that St. Thomas never wasted his thought. He would continue to compose in his mind almost all night. He dictated a question of the *Summa,* an *opusculum,* gave a sermon at the University, and taught his course in the morning. It would take a whole volume merely to list the names of his works. His disciples

[15]William of Tocco writes that, even during the most frightening storms, Thomas strengthened himself with the Sign of the Cross and remained impassible (*quasi pro scuto opponendo se muniens Crucis signo*).

were astonished that he could write so many books in the course of a short twenty years.[16]

Magnanimous, a prodigiously hard worker, Thomas was extremely simple. He practiced our Lord's lesson: "If you do not become as little children, you will not enter the Kingdom of Heaven." In the last two years of his life, when he was in Italy, he was somewhat relieved of that extreme tension of mind that he experienced during the heat of the doctrinal battles. We have noted his detachment from the world and his seclusion, especially from any relationships with women. Yet he experienced and practiced fraternal charity. We often read of his friendship with Bonaventure. The two doctors knew one another, and appreciated one another's work. But history has shown that they could not have been close friends. This friendship is in great part legendary, and those who treat of it can only be certain of its most general aspects. They wanted to give Thomas a friendship he never had, while they ignored the one that really did exist. Thomas simply and spontaneously cultivated an

[16]Only Mozart was as productive. Although he died at the age of thirty-five, Mozart had composed twenty Masses, twenty-two operas, forty-nine symphonies, six cantatas, twenty-five concertos for string and wind instruments, twenty-nine piano concertos, nine quintets, thirty-one quartets, forty-five sonatas for piano and violin, twenty-two sonatas for piano, etc.—a total of more than six hundred works. It is as natural for some geniuses to produce masterpieces as it is for them to breathe.

absolutely intimate and ineffable friendship with his disciple Reginald of Piperno whom he loved as only the saints can love. We strongly believe that, even in Religious houses today, such consentient friendships are unknown. Reginald was the son of Thomas' thought, his friend, confidant, and *domesticus*. He lived in the cell next to the Master's. As a privilege of his office of Regent, Thomas had the use of a little workroom or office. At night, when he had composed some question in his mind, he called Reginald, and both went to work on it. They went back to sleep; and in the morning Thomas would give the signal to rise. Reginald would then serve his Master's Mass, and immediately afterwards, Thomas would serve Mass for his disciple. Their friendship grew deeper and deeper, until they were united as one spirit. Brother Thomas confessed to Reginald, disclosing his least negligences and temptations, confiding the secrets of his visions and ecstasies, commanding that Reginald keep the knowledge of these heavenly revelations to himself. Reginald confessed to his Master, and followed his counsel and advice. When they met difficulties in their work, both went together to the chapel to pray. We have learned of Thomas' most secret visions from Reginald. Finally, Reginald performed the task of infirmarian, and served his master in the refectory, seeing that Thomas lacked nothing, watching that he did not burn himself with a candle while in ecstasy.[17]

Their friendship was more intimate than we can imagine. Only saints are without any natural or spiritual secrets from one another, even in regard to confessional matter. Such a friendship presupposes very pure, very sincere souls, lacking all personal ambition and desire for glory. One day, Thomas almost lost Brother Reginald. They were returning together from Rome to Naples, when both came down with a terrible fever which could not be prevented nor healed. They stopped at the château of Cardinal Richard. Thomas suffered for three days with the fever, and soon recovered. But Reginald's fever became continually worse, and the doctor despaired of his life. Thomas, very sad and upset, seized the relics of St. Agnes which he carried with him, and convinced of their efficacy, suggested that Reginald put them on his chest. The patient believed, and to the great surprise of the doctor, he was cured. Master Thomas recognized this as a miraculous healing, and promised the brothers of the convent of Naples a special meal

[17]William of Tocco writes: "Fr. Raynaldus de Piperno, qui totius vitae ejus meruit esse testis et socius. Cui non solum servivit, ut Magistro discipulus, ut Patri filius, sed ut sancto devotus, circa quem oportebat semper assumere nutricis officium, propter abstractionem quasi continuam, et frequentem ad caelestia mentis raptum, ut sui abstractum ab exterioribus praevenire etiam oporteret de necessariis corporis alimentis" (Boll., *op. cit.*, p. 676).

each year on the feast of St. Agnes. But he could fulfill his promise only once, for his own death was imminent.[18]

[18]This edifying and simple account has the surest guarantees of authenticity. It is told very succinctly by Tolomeo of Lucca who was present. Along with Reginald, and in the latter's absence, Tolomeo was Thomas' socius and confessor. The Master received an ounce of gold from the King for his courses, which he could use to pay for the meal.

Four: THE DEATH OF ST. THOMAS

"Death," wrote Père Lacordaire, "is the term and decisive moment of life. Before death, man appears truly great. And until that solemn, powerful, and fortunate day, he has not yet reached the heights of his greatness. All virtues need the consecration of death to appear in all their brilliance." These words are as true as they are magnificent. History confirms them and teaches us that we must analyze a man's death in order to recognize and determine his character. Père Lacordaire cites the death of Socrates as indicative of his life and mission to Athens. On his deathbed, Taine was reading a page of psychology from Saint-Beuve's *Lundis.* He was the man who wrote to Georges Fonsegrive: "I have never been occupied with anything but psychology." These examples emphasize the point that death usually reveals the dominant preoccupation of man's life. What a great difference there is between the death of these men and that of the saints! The death of a St. Francis of Assisi, a St. Catherine of Siena, a St. Theresa of Avila is sublime. In the words of Pascal, it is of another order, supernatural. St. Thomas' death has all the sublimity of the deaths of these famous mystics. But at the same time, it manifests his true character. We shall attempt to expose the circumstances, conditions, and principles of his death according to an integrated historical method, which will aim at deepening the proportion of natural and mystical causes, without confusing or separating them, and above all, without excluding any of them.

The natural causes of death—sickness, old age, injuries, etc.—are familiar enough that we need only mention them. Among the saints, however, there exist other causes of death which we cannot ignore, much less deny. We need only call upon the testimony of the greatest authority on this subject, St. John of the Cross. This theologian, who was gifted with the richest mystical phenomena and a most penetrating insight into their principles, wrote:

> The death of souls that reach that state [union], although it appears from the natural standpoint to be like that of others, differs greatly in its cause and mode. The death of others may be caused by sickness or old age. But when these [souls in the state of union] die, they may succumb to sickness or old age, but their spirits are drawn from the body by a loving impulse, stronger than any they experienced before, for this time it has the strength and energy necessary to break the web and bear the jewel away.

Although we have quoted only this passage, the whole commentary of John of the Cross in *The Living Flame,* on the verse, "Break the web of this sweet encounter," deserves to be read and meditated upon frequently. According to John of the Cross, the death of the saints who wish to possess God "is the same as that of others from the natural point of view, although it differs considerably in its cause and mode." We can distinguish three different principles in a saint's death: the natural condition, mode, and cause.

As we have said, *natural conditions* are such things as sickness and old age. The *mode* of a mystic's death is sweetness and angelic patience amid even the bitterest sufferings undergone for the love of God. These souls united to God pronounce the most touching and sublime words at the moment of death. Their last words are like a memorial, a hymn of adoration: "And thus the death of such souls is sweeter and more gentle than their whole spiritual life. They die amid particularly delectable encounters of love, like the swan, which sings most melodiously when it is about to die."

Yet it is not sufficient for a pious person to exhibit edifying signs of devotion for his death to be termed mystical. It is also necessary that the *cause* of this death be the love of God, the desire to see or possess him. We touch here on the most delicate point of our question. How is the desire to love God and to be perfectly united with him the cause of death? John of the Cross uses a clever device to illustrate the progressive detachment or separation of the soul from the body. He compares the life of the senses to a web. This web which envelops the soul is so translucent that the mind, alerted by love, can see light shining through from the divinity. By its detachment from creatures, its passive fidelity to receive the light of divine grace, the soul is little-by-little inflamed with the fire of love. Then the flame begins to attack the web which holds it captive. Although this web is a living tissue which repairs injuries, the soul, as it becomes more fervent, gnaws and burns the web which surrounds it, until it grows thinner and more transparent. He writes: "Soon the web seems finer than a spider's." Then the soul discerns, or rather sees, in a divine light that eternal truths and goods alone are real, and that even the most magnificent earthly realities are, in the words of St. Theresa, a sort of cloud, mere useless straw. "The soul is convinced that the things it sees are nothing; it itself is nothing in its own eyes; its God alone is all."

When the soul comes to the point of reducing the body, the chamber, the coil to a mere transparent film, the end of life is near. In an impetuous burst of love for God, whom the soul sees, it breaks the web. St. John of the Cross speaks here of an impact, or more properly, of a rupture. Because of the strength of its love, the soul longs for the end of life.

> The soul knows that it is God's custom to call before their time the souls whom he loves greatly, as in the words of the Wise Man: "He who pleased God was loved; he who lived among sinners was transported, snatched away . . . having become perfect in a short while, he reached the fullness of a long career, for his soul was made pleasing to the Lord, therefore he sped him out of the midst of the wicked" (Wis. 4:10-14).

This is the teaching of St. John of the Cross on the mystical death of souls who have attained the perfection of love here on earth. We cannot help but notice the truth of his words which summarize Christian tradition. It would be a gross error to think that these are merely the expressions of an ethereal idealism or illusory symbolism. The Saint is speaking metaphorically of his own experiences. He assisted at the death of many saints; he studied much; and he was an expert enough psychologist and theologian to be able to distinguish between the natural conditions and mystical causes of such a death. Although they are not apparent to the senses, these are the truest and most genuine spiritual realities. Compared with these shining truths, sensible phenomena are mere unstable shadows. We shall attempt to give an integrated interpretation of the death of the Angelic Doctor, to discover the role of both mystical and natural causes, trying to avoid an exclusive and biased historical method.

We must refer directly to the testimonies of the witnesses at the process of canonization and to the biography of William of Tocco to ascertain the circumstances surrounding the death of St. Thomas.*

The most valuable and authoritative evidence on the subject, the one that can be called the "source of all sources," is given by Bartholomew of Capua. Protonotary of the Kingdom of Sicily, and the Minister of the Interior, Bartholomew of Capua held second place in the kingdom after the King. He knew Thomas personally, and in his work he is careful to tell us the sources of his information. He had heard the confession of John of Guidice, who had confided all his secrets to him. This

---

*When William of Tocco wrote his biography of St. Thomas he was about seventy-five years old. We should not be surprised to find mistakes and confusion in his edition. Père Denifle's remark that William of Tocco "turns everything upside down" is often only too true. The following is a rather curious example of this. In his biography and testimony at the process of canonization, William of Tocco said that, before he died, St. Thomas made his general confession to Peter of Sezze. He claimed to have been informed of the fact by St. Thomas in a dream, and substituted the name of Peter of Sezze for that of Reginald of Piperno. This testimony is totally erroneous. Generally, when Tocco's evidence does not coincide with the testimonies of the other witnesses, we must reject it. The biography of William of Tocco is, nevertheless, a conscientious work. We should not accuse the author of inventing these things; he was subject to the weakness of old age in confusing dates, places, and facts.

Dominican in turn had heard the general confession of Reginald of Piperno, Thomas' intimate friend and companion. Bartholomew of Capua had what might be termed a direct line to the deposit of secrets concerning the Angelic Doctor. What William of Tocco knew, as he himself tells us, he learned in great part from Bartholomew of Capua.

Bartholomew of Capua prefaces his account of St. Thomas' death by relating a vision which has become famous in the lives of the Saints. On December 6, 1273, while celebrating Mass in the chapel of St. Nicholas, Thomas was strangely disturbed (*fuit mira mutatione commotus*). The earliest documents do not mention an ecstasy, but we may infer from his previous experiences that this was a similar event. For example, on Passion Sunday, in the same convent of Naples, while saying Mass, the Saint was enraptured and tears filled his eyes. Some of the brothers tugged at his vestments, imploring him to finish the Mass. Doubtlessly the same thing happened on the feast of St. Nicholas referred to above. But this time, after the Mass, Thomas wrote no more. He no longer dictated. He stopped his work on the *Summa* in the middle of the third part of the Tract on Penance. To our knowledge, St. Thomas had shown no symptoms of physical or mental weakening. Unlike Pascal or Comte, he did not abandon his work only to take it up again and continue it with great difficulty. Thomas Aquinas, active and in full possession of his faculties, suddenly stopped the composition of his masterpiece, the *Summa Theologiae*. The value of this unique and pre-eminent work must be fully appreciated to measure the extraordinary importance of such a decision. We find nothing comparable to it in history. The Dominican Doctor understood better than anyone else what effect his apologetic and doctrinal synthesis might have in the Church. He sacrificed it. He made a sharp, absolutely unforeseen halt, following an ecstatic revelation, a *"mira mutatione"* in the words of the text, or an "impact" as St. John of the Cross terms it.

Reginald of Piperno was disturbed when he found that the Master had given up his dictation, and Reginald urged him to reveal the cause. He called upon a motive most likely to touch the soul of a son of St. Dominic. "Father," he said, "how can you abandon such an important work, which you have undertaken for the glory of God and the enlightenment of souls?" Certainly Reginald, who was no uneducated copyist, but an excellent theologian, who later assumed the distinguished but demanding task of finishing the *Summa,* Reginald, the confidant and collaborator of the Master, had every right to seek the cause of this abrupt interruption. He thought that Thomas suffered from the strain of his great intellectual activity (*ne propter multum studium aliquam incurrisset amentiam*). Subsequent events showed the Saint to be more and more removed from sensible realities, while at the same time remaining entirely lucid in matters of the spirit.

Nevertheless we would expect, and history must confirm, that this sort of moral weakness in St. Thomas, caused principally by mystical experience, be accompanied by a great physical lassitude. Planning to rest, or so advised by Reginald, the Saint decided to visit his sister, the Countess of San Severino, whom he loved tenderly (*quam caritative diligebat*). The trip was exhausting, and the Saint arrived at his destination only with great difficulty (*magna cum difficultate*). When he reached the Castle of San Severino, he hardly spoke to his sister. The Countess, considerably disturbed, asked Reginald: "What has happened, Thomas seems to be in a stupor, he will not talk to me?" Reginald answered: "Since the feast of St. Nicholas he has been in this state; and he has written nothing." It was then that Reginald compelled the Saint to confide his reason for abandoning the *Summa*. Thomas made him vow by his faith in the Living God, his fidelity toward the Order, and his fraternal charity, not to reveal until after his death the intimate secret he was about to disclose. He added: "Everything I have written seems to me like so much straw compared to the truths which I have seen, and which have been revealed to me."

Soon afterwards, St. Thomas departed for Naples, leaving the Countess in the deepest desolation. It is obvious that Thomas' sister would not have been so upset if a profound change had not taken place in her brother's physical and moral condition. Nevertheless Brother Thomas was not afflicted with a common sickness. Large, powerful, and heavy, his stoutness hid a dangerous weakness. The type of mortification which he had undergone for his life's work could only increase this mysterious weariness. Could not the physical depression which comes from an absolute, transcendent detachment from all reality, from all human science, induce sickness and death? The Countess of San Severino, inspired by love for her brother, had good cause for being upset.

Master Thomas Aquinas had been asked, in a personal letter from Pope Gregory X, to attend the new Council of Lyons. Thomas finished preparations during the month of January, 1274. Such a long voyage in the heart of winter must have been extremely difficult. But the Saint set out, concerned only with obedience. Because of his size and weakness, the Master traveled on muleback. We learn from Tolomeo of Lucca that he suffered from a wound in his leg. He wished to pass through Aquino to take a last look at his childhood home and to console his family. Père Mortier conjectures that Reginald sent ahead to the members of his family the disquieting news of Thomas' condition. When at last he arrived at Aquino, the abbot of Monte Cassino sent a letter inviting him to visit the abbey.

Abbot Bernard Ayglier, a friend of Thomas, called on him to help the monks of Monte Cassino who were troubled by discussions concerning predestination and free will. Despite this important reason and the requests of his friend, Thomas declined the invitation. In his letter to the Abbot, the Saint excused himself because of the fast and long Lenten Office. But this was only a pretext. Compared with the length of his voyage, the detour to the abbey would have been insignificant. Traveling must have become very tiring for the Master. His family and companions probably seriously doubted that he would ever arrive at Lyons. In fact, St. Thomas continued his journey for barely two more days, covering only about fifteen leagues.

Leaving Aquino, he set out toward Terracina; from there he took the Borgo Nuovo road. Thomas was so wrapped in contemplation that he was unaware of his injury when he collided with the overhanging limb of a tree. His companions, Reginald of Piperno, William, the Dean of Teano, and his nephew, Roffredo, rushed forward and asked how badly he was hurt. Thomas answered, "A little." Nevertheless Reginald, who was an infirmarian, knew that the only way to interrupt his ecstatic train of thought was to distract him. So he started talking about the Council. "You will attend the Council where much good will be done for the Church, our Order, and the Kingdom of Sicily." As is customary when talking to a sick person,

Reginald spoke freely. Nevertheless Thomas remained strangely silent and answered succinctly. His words fell one-by-one, heavy with meaning, almost as if he wanted to engrave the memorable sentences in metal. He answered: "God wishes to do much good there." Not to be discouraged by his master's brevity, Reginald said: "You and Bonaventure will be named cardinals, and will be the glory of the two Orders." Then Thomas answered Reginald: "In no state whatever can I be more helpful to our Order than the one I am in now." Reginald answered: "Father, I was not speaking of your advantage but of the common good." This time Thomas cut him short. "Assure yourself that I shall go on exactly as I am." Roffredo told this incident to Bartholomew of Capua. St. Thomas had always feared being raised to a high ecclesiastical office. He prayed earnestly that God would allow him to remain a simple Mendicant Friar. He was confident that his wish would be granted.

When Thomas Aquinas arrived at the home of his niece, at Maenza, his weariness grew worse; and it soon became evident to all that his condition was critical. Only now did Thomas reveal the cause of his illness. We need not think that the Saint suddenly revealed the symptoms of a well-defined disease. In this matter we have a more competent witness than Bartholomew of Capua. We refer here to the Cistercians, particularly Peter of Montesangiovanni. This man was the abbot of Fossanova and a highly influential Religious, who came to visit Thomas at Maenza and remained with him until his death. He mentions several times that St. Thomas' sickness began at the castle of Maenza. The symptoms of this sickness were an extreme lassitude and weakness. During the four days he spent at Maenza, St. Thomas still celebrated the Sacrifice of the Mass with great devotion and a flowing of tears. However, his appetite began to disappear entirely. The episode of the herring took place at this time. We learn also at this time that, besides Reginald, a Dominican named James of Salerno was also accompanying Thomas.

After four or five days at Maenza, the Cistercians returned to the abbey of Fossanova, taking Thomas with them. The account indicates that both Thomas and the others traveled on muleback. Brother Nicholas, Abbot of Fossanova in July of 1319, reports that Thomas was heard to say, "If the Lord has chosen this time for me, it is better that I be found in a religious house than the castle of seculars." Most of the witnesses made a point of mentioning his words as he entered the abbey: "Here is the place of my final rest, I will stay here, because I have chosen it." The Religious of Fossanova interpreted this as a sort of will. They were especially concerned that the relics of the Saint should remain in their monastery. Strangely enough, some reported that the event took place in the parlor of the monastery; others mention the choir of the Church; others name the door near the entrance. Bartholomew of Capua says that, as Thomas entered the monastery, he leaned on the doorpost and said: "Haec requies mea in saeculum saeculi, hic habitabo quoniam elegi eam."

William of Tocco tells us that the Cistercians arranged the abbot's own room for St. Thomas. These faithful sons of St. Benedict showed every possible kindness to the famous son of St. Dominic. Nicholas, the Abbot of Fossanova, tells the incident of the logs. When asked by the inquisitors how he learned of this event, Abbot Nicholas answered that he had been present, and had seen and heard it for himself.

> The monks of the monastery, because of the great devotion they had for Thomas Aquinas, and because of his reputation for holiness, carried logs for the fireplace. They thought that it was hardly fitting to have animals render this service for such a famous man. Each time that Thomas heard the monks coming to the room where he was sleeping, he would pull himself up protesting: "Who am I that holy men should bring me my firewood?"

After relating this episode in such detail, we would expect Abbot Nicholas to include the events surrounding St. Thomas' commentary on the Canticle of Canticles. But he passes over it in silence. The other Cistercians do not refer to the commentary either. This occasion would have been an appropriate place to show the knowledge, profound piety, and sanctity of the man they were trying to canonize. Must we conclude that St. Thomas did not comment on the Canticle of Canticles on his deathbed? We do not think so. Further on, we shall investigate the silence of the witnesses. Let it suffice for now to mention that William of Tocco's account is very sure and precise.

Thomas remained for a month with the Cistercians of Fossanova. In his last days, he felt even weaker, and asked for the Blessed Sacrament as Viaticum. The Abbot and monks brought it to him devotedly and with solemnity. According to William of Tocco, Thomas was lying down and was very weak. But his soul showed its characteristic strength. He stood up and walked toward his Lord, his eyes filled with tears. When the Abbot asked him the customary question, whether he believed that the Consecrated Host was really the Son of God, born of the Virgin Mary, Thomas made his profession of love for Jesus in a firm voice and with an obviously conscious devotion. Most witnesses testified to his fervor as he knelt before the Sacrament speaking his feelings of devotion. According to the monastic custom, all the Religious were assembled in the large room of the Abbot. They even filled the connecting corridors. The lay brothers, three or four visiting Franciscans, and the

Dominicans in Thomas' party were among them. There were about one hundred monks present. In a loud voice the Saint spoke strong and magnificent praise to the Host of Salvation. The old Abbot, Peter Montesangiovanni, who witnessed the scene, remembered his words. "I have taught much about this most Holy Body of Christ and the other sacraments. I subject all my teaching to the Roman Church." Bartholomew of Capua and William of Tocco add these words:

> I have received you, price of the redemption of my soul; I have received you, Viaticum of my pilgrimage; for your love I have studied, kept vigils, worked, preached, and taught. I have never spoken against you, unless it was in my ignorance. And I don't wish to insist on my opinions; but if I have said anything wrong, I leave it all to the correction of the Roman Church.

Viaticum was brought to St. Thomas on March 4, 1274. He lived for three more days. On the morning of March the seventh, he received Extreme Unction. He was still fully conscious, since, according to John of Piperno, he answered distinctly the prayers for the dying. Reginald, who heard his general confession, and Peter of Montesangiovanni were at his side. St. Thomas Aquinas died in the arms of a Dominican and a Cistercian, on March 7, 1274; he was in his fiftieth year.

This is what the records relate of the circumstances preceding and accompanying St. Thomas' death. Even a superficial study reveals that neither the witnesses nor the early biographers mention the name of St. Thomas' sickness. J. Carle, the author of a little-known life of the Saint, offers this suggestion. "We are surprised at the silence of Dominican authors about the nature of St. Thomas' sickness. Nevertheless, from the moment he breathed his last, rumor spread through Italy that he was poisoned." The chronicle of Monte Cassino records the public charge of poisoning. Dante echoes this opinion in the well-known lines of his *Il Purgatorio*:

"Charles came to Italy, and for amends,
Made a victim of Conradino; and then
Thrust Thomas back to heaven, for amends."

Villani accused the physician of Charles of Anjou of poisoning St. Thomas. It seems that Charles had been rude to the Saint's niece. And it was feared that Thomas would complain of this at the Council of Lyons. Tolomeo of Lucca, a considerable authority, states that someone poisoned Thomas' wound. This hypothesis is certainly only a legend. But, like most legends, it poses a problem which is not easy to solve. It appears quite evident that, if St. Thomas had died of a common or well-known sickness, the people of that time would not have dreamed up the theory that he was poisoned. For example, if Thomas had suffered from a fever or malaria, the witnesses would not have mistaken it for another disease; and they would certainly have reported it. In the canonization process itself they speak of a continuous fever. They say that the doctor administered remedies for it. But as for St. Thomas they speak only of his lassitude, extreme weakness, and lack of appetite. We search in vain for the usual terms describing a fever (*patiebatur febrim, febricitabat*), as we find in the case of St. Dominic, Blessed Reginald, and St. Catherine of Siena. The fact that St. Thomas had no fever indicates that he succumbed physically to some mental exhaustion.

Most historians have ascribed the death of the Angelic Doctor to exhaustion from his immense work, his constant application, and his continual ecstatic experiences. This explanation is partially acceptable to us. However, to give as full an account as possible we must keep the mystical explanation in view. How does the human mind operate when a Thomas or a Catherine of Siena dictates in ecstasy? Is there a dichotomy operative between the higher and lower mental centers? What fatigue results from it? St. Theresa, in her last *Moradas,* says that the soul by its visions and outbursts of love for God is always on the point of leaving the body. She writes:

> Two things on the spiritual road are a peril to life. First of all, there is pain, because it poses a great and real threat of death. The second is excessive rejoicing and delight, which can be carried to such an extreme that the slightest thing would be enough to drive it [the soul] out of the body.

When the saint speaks of the wound caused by the "heavenly thrust," she writes:

> Life is certainly in great danger. As brief as the martyrdom may be, it has the effect of making the limbs seem disjointed. The pulse is so weak that it looks as if the body is ready to give up its hold on the soul. For two or three days afterward, the person is in great pain, and scarcely has the strength to write. In fact, the body seems to me to be weaker than it was before.

Why did St. Thomas' soul remain in his body even after his constant ecstasies? As St. Theresa said: "The body is always weaker than it was before." Why did an irreversible weakness not set in after the sublime ecstasy of December 6, 1273? St. Thomas was very aware of the short period he would have to live after this vision. This is why he said: "Brother Reginald, the end of my work has come, and I hope that the end of my life will come as soon as the end of my teaching (*Venit finis scrip-*

turae meae . . . et sicut doctrinae, sic cito finis erit et vitae)." Therefore we must not separate Thomas' death from the vision. The final illness of the Angelic Doctor began with the ecstasy of December 6, 1273.

Some have objected that Thomas wrote or at least dictated after the vision. As we have seen, he received a letter from the Abbot of Monte Cassino inviting him to the monastery. The Master refused the invitation, and resorted to solving the Abbot's problem in writing. This letter fills less than two pages of the Vivés edition. If Thomas wrote or dictated this letter, would we have to conclude that Bartholomew of Capua and William of Tocco were misled, and mislead us when they say that Thomas never wrote after the famous vision? Were this true, the alleged interruption of his theological works following the vision would only be a pious legend. But Bartholomew of Capua repeats the very words of Reginald of Piperno; and William of Tocco asserts the fact in two different places in the Saint's life. It is a witnessed fact of history that, after the sixth of December, the Angelic Doctor ended his theological career. A two-page letter can hardly be considered a continuation or return to the abandoned theological work. Père Mortier, who has carefully reconstructed the life of St. Thomas, and who mentions the letter to the Abbot of Monte Cassino, does not seem to feel that this letter could be used as evidence that the Saint returned to his work after the vision (*Suspendit organa scriptionis suae*).

But St. Thomas is also supposed to have delivered a commentary on the Canticle of Canticles to the monks of Fossanova. We would be mistaken to call this explanation of the Canticle of Canticles given by St. Bernard to the Cistercians of Fossanova a commentary in the usual sense of the word. William of Tocco, the only biographer who mentions it, has already said that Thomas was very weak (*amodum debilis*). Sitting in an armchair or resting in his bed, the Saint agreed to interpret the Canticle of Canticles briefly for several of the monks who asked him to do so. This commentary was, in the well-chosen words of his biographer, only a memorial, a remembrance, a tribute to his learning. Naturally there is a great temptation to compare this commentary to St. Bernard's. But the analogy is rather farfetched. If, during the last month he spent at the abbey of Fossanova, St. Thomas had commented methodically on the Canticle of Canticles for the whole community, the silence of the Cistercians assembled at the process of canonization would be inexplicable. We must, then, accept William of Tocco's account. St. Thomas offered these brief observations to a few of the more learned monks. He did not compose a theological tract. And it would be rash to conclude from this that the Saint resumed his theological works after his vision.

In the words of the Saint himself, the vision of December the sixth truly marked both the end of his work and the decline of his physical strength.

Is it possible to determine at least approximately the nature of this vision? To appreciate its sublimity we must first of all realize that the Saint himself had been favored with visions during his entire life of study. He had often been raised up from the ground. He spoke intimately with the Apostles Peter and Paul. Twice, Christ approved his Eucharistic doctrine. We can hardly doubt that the Angelic Doctor had attained the seventh mansion which St. Theresa describes, the perfect union with God in which the mystic's soul, as if outside the body, enjoys the vision of the Trinity. Such a vision would not have rendered him powerless to finish the *Summa*. On the contrary, it would have encouraged him to complete this unique and incomparable masterpiece of Christian theology. The vision which made him lay down his pen, which made him call all he had written straw, empty and without substance, was undoubtedly of a more elevated nature than those he had previously experienced.

St. John of the Cross, analyzing the highest mystical favors, the ecstasies of love, remarks that they are ordinarily given "to souls destined to transmit their spirit and virtue to a group of disciples." In other words, these favors are given to the founders and foundresses of Religious Orders. But, speaking of a still more transcendent vision, he says that it is reserved for a few souls who have represented God and the Church, and have taught the articles of faith.

> Visions of immaterial substances, such as the Divine Being . . . are not proper to this life, and no mortal could be favored by them. If God wishes to communicate them to a soul in their essence, this soul would leave the flesh and earthly life. So God answered Moses when he asked to see the Divine Essence: *Non videbit me homo et vivit* (No man sees me and lives).

As we see, such visions are incompatible with life. We might point out that the manifestations of the Divine Substance with which Paul, Moses, and Elijah were favored are very rare, so much so that God confers them only on exceptional men who represent the sources of the Church's spirit and Divine Law in a special way.

But the famous Carmelite mystic teaches us that the highest, rarest favors given to the founders or foundresses of Religious Orders are "in proportion to the importance of the doctrines and the spirit that they have had to communicate to those following after them." Not being received in this life in "a clear and precise way by the understanding, they return to the stage of spiritual feelings; *perception is made by a knowledge of love.*" For this reason, it is proper to say that these people die of love. But, according to our own mystical Doctor, by an absolutely extraordinary grace that is rarely found in history, God can show himself with his heavenly court, the angels and blessed souls, "in a clear and precise fashion." This vision will not be knowledge of love, but, properly speaking, a vision, and it is conferred "on exceptional men who have represented the sources of the Church's spirit and the Divine Law in a special way."

It seems to us that the highest vision of St. Thomas—and we call it the highest not precisely because it was the last, but because it marked the end of his theological work and his earthly involvement—was a vision of light rather than a vision of love. First of all, in the explanation the Saint gave to Brother Reginald, he uses only the verb *to see*: "After what I *saw*, all I have written seems to me nothing but straw." As is fitting with the most intellectual of Christian doctors, intelligence played a greater part in his ecstasies than did his will. We are not attempting to say that the rarest and most exceptional visions of love experienced by the mystics have discouraged them from writing. It seems to us that St. Thomas Aquinas, who has acquired an incomparable doctrinal leadership in the Church, should rightly be placed among the exceptional men St. John of the Cross refers to as having "represented the sources of the Spirit of the Church and the Divine Law in a special way."

These providential geniuses, predestined to give a rule of faith and life to thousands of souls, should be divinely authorized. As the Pharisee put it, Moses was believed by the Israelites because "he had seen God." As a sanction of his teachings to the Corinthians, St. Paul appealed to his vision on the road to Damascus and to his ecstasy to the third heaven. It appears entirely possible that St. Thomas, whose teaching would be made the law of the Church for many centuries, would have been favored with a vision of light far superior to the ecstasies given to saints like Dominic or Catherine of Siena. The comparison of Thomas with Moses and St. Paul is not a new one. William of Tocco, writing before the process of canonization, remarked:

> In the same way that God revealed truths surpassing the human intellect to those who were the sources of the Law, to Moses who brought the Law of Justice to the Jews, and to Paul who preached the Law of Grace to the Gentiles, so also he revealed the supernatural mysteries to Blessed Thomas Aquinas. Thomas received the book of the Old and New Law from him who sits on the throne of glory. He opened and explained them clearly for all Christianity.

Finally, we must consider the providential importance of this vision. It is often used as an example by preachers and spiritual directors. It will always remain a valuable lesson for both the simplest and most learned of the faithful. St. Thomas Aquinas, after an extraordinary ecstasy, some months before his death, called all his writings straw. What a masterly and painful lesson to inflict on the pride of spirit, the knowledge which would masquerade as prayer or contemplation! This lesson is of universal and eternal importance. And it ought to be the subject of meditation. It teaches us to search, according to our meager talents, for truth in the light of a Christian spirit shaped in humility and enriched by prayer, and not solely by an intellectual approach.

"They succumb to some sickness or to old age," wrote St. John of the Cross, "but what detaches the soul from the body will only be a bursting forth, an aspiration of love." We must modify this text a little to apply it to the special case of Thomas Aquinas. What broke the web of sensible life surrounding the Angelic Doctor, refined for many years by daily ecstasies, was this glaring vision, a ray of the Light of Glory. And because it did not produce precisely a burst of love but a burst of divine light, it slowly extinguished the Saint's life, exactly three months after he set aside his work on the *Summa*. It is not we who claim that Thomas saw God, but William of Tocco who presented the idea to John XXII to obtain his Master's canonization. Neither the Pope, nor the examiners of the cause, nor the Dominicans, nor those who read this biography thought the suggestion foolhardy. What would they have said had they foreseen the doctrinal leadership Thomas would acquire in the next six centuries? Taking up William's idea and adding what we know of subsequent history, we can agree with him when he says:

> This is the Moses of sacred doctrine, who spoke face to face with God, who understood so clearly the divinely-revealed truths that he seemed to see the Trinity visible in the Scripture where they are hidden. This is the Angelic Doctor who was constantly in ecstasy, who discovered mysteries so superior to the realm of human intelligence that his soul was absorbed in the Divinity. In awe before the sublimity of the revelation received at the end of his life, he scorned all he had written and abandoned his work.

And we add: He who was the mystical Doctor died shortly after having contemplated God in a vision of light.